# MERCEDES
*Magic*

## THE STORY OF THE 1989 LE MANS RACE

**KEN WELLS**

# Hydro Aluminium in the World Sports-Prototype Championship.

Sponsor: Hydro Aluminium, Team: Brun, Car: Porsche 962-005 BM, Class C1, Drivers: Harald Huysman (N), Stanley Dickens (S)

((( HYDRO ALUMINIUM

# CONTENTS

# A WINTER'S TALE

**I**T WAS A GLORIOUSLY golden afternoon. The sun was shining and the birds were singing, a strong hint of summer in the air. Unseasonably high temperatures belied the fact that it was still early February.

Up on the beach young girls frolicked, the guys pitting their skills and sailboards against dark Atlantic rollers. Retirees, wintering down south far from northern chills, watched them with envy, remembering the salad days of their own lost youth, their peace shattered only by the shrill sounds of youthful exuberance as yet another wave crashed against the wide sandy shore. Those minor distractions apart, all seemed at peace in the world.

As it did five miles away where, thirty years ago, on what was barren marsh land adjacent to the local airport, 'Big' Bill France had built a shrine, not to any Sun God but to the Kings of Speed, a temple dedicated to the internal combustion engine. This was the Daytona International Speedway and the upcoming weekend would witness its annual 24 Hours sportscar classic.

All along the pitlane there was not much going on, the first practice session of the new season still a full quarter of an hour away. Everyone was taking it easy, mechanics making last minute adjustments to their charges, media types snatching a word here or a photo there, the drivers – all kitted up with nowhere yet to go – soaking up those hot early afternoon rays.

Seated on the wall, dressed in his red race suit, was the ever ebullient Bruce Leven, a man who had literally made money from muck with his Bayside Disposal company of garbage collectors. So much so that it had enabled him to purchase a couple of Porsche 962s, both of which were sitting out front waiting to be fired into action. The minutes ticked away, quietly and without drama.

The next two pits were consigned to Jim Busby's BF Goodrich team, the same folk who had given Jaguar such a good run to the chequered flag last year. Resplendent in bright Miller livery, Busby's two Porsches awaited the arrival of their pilots, Britain's Derek Bell joining Bob Wollek and young John Andretti in one, while the other would contain John's uncle and cousin, Mario

and Michael Andretti. The father and son driving force from Nazareth in Pennsylvania had long since taken on a mantle of near divinity as motor racing's First Family and their presence was awaited with interest.

As the hour of judgement approached, into the pits they came, Mario and Micheal leading John (son of Mario's twin brother Aldo) with a whole entourage of minders and minions, media folk and hangers-on trailing in their wake. Buttoned up ready for action like the modern day gladiators they are, it was, said one erudite commentator, just like former President Reagan entering a press conference: all very regal without putting on airs.

Leven's reaction was spontaneous. Jumping up, he grabbed his helmet, turned to the assembled audience and exclaimed: "Oh boy, the Andrettis are here. *NOW* we can go racing!"

As everyone else dissolved into laughter the A-team cruised on by, their faces showing no emotion, their dark 'shades' giving away no glint of recognition, not so much as a sideways glance. It was as if a serene ocean liner had passed a noisy dinghy.

Down at the far end of the pit lane things were much more subdued. Most

of the attention thereabouts was being focussed on the three TWR Castrol Jaguars which sat it out in the noon-day sun preparing to defend their honour. Last year they had turned up for their first race in the IMSA series – at its blue riband and toughest event – as the new boys in town. They left victorious; striking fear into the hearts of all the other competitors that the XJR9 V12s would sweep everything before them as the season unfolded. They didn't.

Nissan did – almost. Don Devendorf's Electramotive equipe are American down to their cylinder blocks, only the historical origins of their engine having anything but the remotest direct

link with any product of Japan. Missing the early season rounds at Daytona then Miami, their GTP ZX-Turbo had outrun everyone else almost everywhere thereafter, winning nine of twelve championship starts.

The thing was, however, that the Nissan had never before raced for more than three hours at a time, all its accumulated IMSA title chasing successes of 1988 totalling less than the duration of this single event so not many people held out much hope for what someone described as the red-white-and-blur. It would be fast but lucky to last until midnight went the general consensus of opinion. Time would tell.

Always around at the end are the Porsches. Although overshadowed these last twelve months by the likes of Nissan in America, Mercedes in Europe and Jaguars everywhere, nonetheless they are still formidable beasts over the Daytona distance. Rather than be sprint cars which do the longer distances, Porsches are endurance racers which often do sprints. The difference is subtle, the consequences immense.

Twenty-eight times these past two decades they had shown everyone the way home in the two-day affairs, be it here or at Le Mans, often capturing both

in the same season. Indeed, 1988 was the first time since the early Seventies that they had won neither. Porsche were out for revenge.

There were nine of them. Undoubtably some were only making up the numbers when it came to having any realistic chance at outright victory, both the Wynn's and Freedom/Andale versions falling into that category, as could Reinhold Joest's entry for Jean-Louis Ricci, Claude Ballot-Lena and the under-rated Frank Jelinski. Nor was that Leven fellow likely to be first to the chequer, teaming up with his pal Rob Dyson to form 'The Cruise Brothers'. That said it all.

*In the golden glow of sunset, Porsche #67 heads through the infield en route to victory.*

Bayside's other entry, the #86 Texaco Havoline car, looked far more promising, listing as it did the combined talents of Klaus Ludwig, James Weaver and Sarel van Der Merwe on its door.

Close by, if sponsor decals ensured success Walter Brun would be unbeatable, the car he was sharing with Hans Stuck and Oscar Larrauri buried under a veritable lexicon of logos. Resembling a mobile 'Scrabble' board, nevertheless it spelled out a potential winner.

The Torno-Momo example seemed naked by comparison. Led by Mauro Baldi – pole sitter last year – anything could happen to the red and green machine. Unfortunately, it did.

And last but by no means least came Busby, a quick examination of the facts showing his team to be first amongst equals.

The quiet Californian had been picked to take the mandate of the late Al Holbert, killed in an air crash last September. His would now be the favoured entry of Porsche Motorsport North America and so the nearest thing to a 'works' Porsche entry. He even had Al's beer money from last season as well as the famous Holbert Racing 962-HR7 to go alongside his own Chapman chassised 962-108 with its revised aerodynamics. What more could the guy wish for in life?

Whatever the answer, he got Andretti and Andretti. With their infrequent forays into sports car racing the Indycar heroes bring with them the same aura, chaos and hype as would Ian Botham opening the batting for a village XI or Joe Montana going 'Little League'. Treated by most people – with one notable exception! – as if to the manna born, it is they who got the star treatment, it is they who got Porsche 962-HR7.

Yet sportscar racing has its own heroes and Derek Bell is paramount amongst them. Five times a winner at Le Mans and twice in its Florida equivelent, teamed with Wollek and young Andretti, John Andrew, you could not help thinking that this ultra talented trio of Bell, Bob and 'The Boy' were being dismissed as the B-team. But B stands for best and time was on their side. . .

From somewhere amongst this bunch would come the likely winner, the rare sight of a Mazda rotary with its familiar less than friendly cry of the banshees, unlikely to mark a first outing here with outright victory. But we'd also heard *THAT* before!

Further down the road, the great Dan Gurney had brought along not his new AAR Eagle but a Group C Toyota 88C, citing the new car to be tested but untried for such an arduous event.

Of the other GTP cars at rest on that hallowed piece of tarmac that peaceful afternoon, only the brace of Spices looked likely to cause much concern to the big boys, the Ball Brothers' example immaculate in its Jiffy Lube colour scheme, the bright Old Spice livery

almost apt on the new 'works' Pontiac V8 version for Costas Los/Jeff Kline/Dieter Quester.

Making up the numbers, the class of '89 was completed by a custard coloured Fabcar – looking better than it went – and Tom Milner's stable of similarly hued aging Ford Probes. Rumours abounded that Milner had been offered a prince's ransom to sell his charges, most people reckoning he should have taken the money and run. As things would turn out, he would probably have gone quicker than the cars did. . .

So the scene was set that bright winter's day, the GTP top rankers sharing a crowded pitlane with many a varied contender from other spheres, most noticable amongst them being the magnificent Mercury Cougars and Capri V8s prepared by Jack Roush, their 180 mph straight-line speed no slouch in anybody's terms. Nor was the fearsome Mandeville RX7 likely to be left hanging around waiting for anybody with its rotary screamer, Brian Redman amongst those destined to handle this brutal beast. All in all there were sixty-eight cars destined to start Saturday's great race, the fast and the furious, the flotsam and the jetsam – but only one would be the winner.

As everyone pondered their fates under that blazing Florida sky a faraway clock struck the top of the hour. The time had come. And as the man said: *NOW* we can go racing!

Jaguar, the defending champions of The Big D, had hardly gotten started before they stopped again. Only a few minutes into the opening session John Nielsen came hurtling over the start-finish line at a full 200 mph, hooked hard left past the pits en route to the tricky infield section and promptly had the right front wheel fall off!

It was not the beginning they would have chosen. Saturday's would be even worse.

TWR had brought three cars to the race, their chassis plates indicating they were the same tubs for the same race numbers as last time, i.e. #60 being –288 and thus last year's winner, #61 showing –388 and #66 with –188. Although visually similar to 1988, there had been many modifications beneath the skin especially regarding engines and brakes, but for outsiders only the removal of the roof mounted airscoop, mesh covered side ducting and bigger wheels (now a full eighteen inches) showed much to differentiate today's challenger from yesterday's champion.

It was the drivers who had changed. Alongside the familiar seasoned campaigners of Nielsen, Jan Lammers, Raul Boesel and Davy Jones came many a familiar face in unfamiliar circumstances, Andy Wallace, hero of Le Mans, getting his reward for a job well done by being contracted for a full season this time.

Price Cobb and Derek Daly were renewing an acquaintance which had previously seen them in XJR9s only at La Sarthe last June at which time Martin Donnelly had been 'just' another highly talented F3 driver awaiting the big break. He got it soon afterwards, first in F3000 then aboard the Lloyd Porsche, and now stood there looking the part in his Castrol overalls, preparing to drive a factory backed Jaguar in one of the most prestigious motor races in the world. A Lotus F.1. testing contract safely tucked into his back pocket, the Ulsterman had certainly come a long way in a short time.

As could also be said of veteran Patrick Tambay, albeit by a different route. The French former Grand Prix winner for Ferrari has more recently taken to doing the Paris-Dakar Raid. Whatever the next few days might throw at him, it would be nothing compared to the Sahara or the Tenere.

Two pits along, their neighbourliness interrupted only by a humble GTU outfit, Nissan were throwing everything into the fray. Not privileged to be given a spot in the lock-up garages of Gasoline Alley, the IMSA pace setters were normally to be found out in the general paddock, sharing space with a clapped out Tiga Mazda and much less besides. Now, with their two splendid charges on pit road, they were the equal of everybody, maybe better. . .

After the ninety minutes of the preliminary practice session, Daytona custom is for a short break then Pole Day qualification to immediately follow, which it duly did. Judged on the best of only two flying laps, although tomorrow would still leave time for the rest to sort themselves out, today secured the front row and the Nissans meant to get it for themselves.

Some came and others went, a variety of sports car racing's finest all vying for top honour in the afternoon sun. Then came Jan Lammers, seventh out with

Jeff Kline's very impressive showing aboard the Spice Pontiac to beat, the stocky little Nederlander fully living up to his subtitle as 'The Flying Dutchman'. In a lap with all the flair but none of the wall-clipping moments of last year – well, not quite so heavily anyway! – he turned in a magnificent 1m39.855s to leap to the front of the queue, climbing from the #60 car to the instant adulation of his team mates.

As their hero perched himself high in the mobile command module Jaguar time keepers call home from home, two cars later out went Chip Robinson in Nissan #84. Things were getting serious.

He was soon back again, but not soon enough, the 1987 Daytona winner and IMSA champion, a mere 23/1000ths shy of the Jaguar. Close, but no cigar. The Castrol crew cheered again.

Next it was Derek Patrick Daly, fractions slower still, the tension and the temperature mounting in the pitlane as the afternoon sun, by now dipping low behind the serried ranks of grandstands, lost its own heat.

Then came Geoff Brabham and the thermometers reached new heights, the reigning series champion ready to put the matter beyond all doubt. Completing his warm-up lap, he blasted around the infield, down the back straightaway, through the chicane, around the banking, home sweet home. Crowding around the nearest convenient monitor, necks craning to see, everyone stared in eager anticipation awaiting the news, the blinking of a microchip soon revealing a 1m39.182s. He'd done it!

And it wasn't the Castrol crew who were cheering now!

Price Cobb nor any of the other late chargers managed to top the son of 'Black Jack' and so over the next day gradually the grid sorted itself out, Electramotive retaining first and third, Jaguar holding second, seventh and eighth. Best for Porsche was Brun #3 in fourth, Ludwig next up for the Texaco star, sharing the third row with the Old Spice car. Completing the top twelve came the Andrettis and the Mazda, the Freedom/Andale machine and the other Miller car, Derek Bell heard to complain as to how Costas Los had blown him into the weeds at one point aboard the Spice V8. Things did not bode too well for 'Dinger'. They boded even worse for those that followed him. . .

Race day dawned as warm as any. Everyone had been busy, going over and over their preparations, tightening this and rechecking that. Down at the Jaguar encampment yesterday, the mechanics had jokingly muttered that they were changing an engine for no good reason

*Spiderman meets the Skoal Bandit. Yet again the McCall Camaro lost a probable GTO class win in the final hours.*

other than that they had not done so for a fortnight. Elsewhere, others went about similar tasks, the clock ticking on, time running out.

That was yesterday and yesterdays count for nothing in this game, Jan Lammers telling at least one television interviewer on Saturday morning that the difference between Le Mans and Daytona was that that was then and this is now, his attitude epitomising TWR resolve not to rest on past glories. Today is what matters and as the cars were pushed out onto the pitlane the two Nissans, like grand dames at a pantomime, were last to take up their places, upstaging everyone else best they could. Ahead of the pack, it was a position they intended to maintain.

The start got underway eight minutes late, Arie Luyendyk, the popular Indycar driver, not keeping anybody waiting any further by blasting the pole sitting 'Brabham' Nissan into the lead from flagfall, his compatriot Lammers in hot pursuit. Larrauri – already suffering serious braking difficulties – and Ludwig were next up as they hurtled through the infield, former Can-Am champion Michael Roe fifth aboard the second Nissan. This car, it had been decreed, would be sacrificed to the cause after the first hour as Electramotive only had the resources to maintain a vigil over a single contender. So it would bow out soon – but not before making its mark on the eventual outcome.

*Kicking up the dust, Nissan #83 gave this view to the world for nearly nineteen hours.*

Ludwig, however, was on a charge. By the time the leaders made it onto the banking Klaus had left the Argentinian behind and proceeded to take the Jaguar with a low pass, Luyendyk now fifty metres to the good. It did not last. Down the back straightaway they went, Klaus gaining all the while before diving inside the Nissan as they entered the chicane, coming around to complete the first lap with a clear advantage. The man from Bonn reckoned the special bodywork designed by his own company made the Leven car the fastest Porsche on Daytona's straights. With speed like that nobody was likely to argue.

Someone travelling much slower was Michael Roe. As was Derek Daly. Not a matter of shillelaghs at dawn but rather a case of red mist in the afternoon, the Irish pair had tangled heavily, blaming each other for the indiscretion. Pitting to inspect battle damage, the Jaguar was first to rejoin but not for long, returning only a single lap later. As its crew pushed the stricken machine behind their pits, closer inspection soon revealed a suspension arm pulled out of the carbon fibre tub. In the immediacy of the event it was irreparable, the race for Donnelly and Tambay over before it had began. As it was for the squad of great British mechanics flown in especially for the occasion, Car #66 being 'their' car. They had all come a long way for nothing.

The battle raged on. Ludwig was still in front on the helter-skelter while Lammers, having gotten by Luyendyk, had Arie tailing him like a shadow. Fighting their own private Dutch battle while also attempting to take on the Havoline car, both of them actually hauled Ludwig in and got ahead briefly, but not for long, Klaus soon fighting back. And such was their pace that within only a few hectic laps they also had the slow goers to contend with, Jan once straight-lining the chicane as he attempted to lap up backmarkers, kicking dust high into the afternoon sky. Traffic, so many cars and drivers of such differing abilities on a relatively small track (the 3.56 mile course being less than half its Le Mans equivalent) is one of the biggest problems of Daytona. The other is the night.

By the time darkness descended over Florida the position had changed dramatically. Ludwig handed over to Weaver, the Brit to 'Super Van', whereupon problems immediately set in. A broken throttle linkage dropped the car sixteen laps, enough to put it out of immediate contention although not the overall picture, there still being a long way to go.

Meanwhile, not going anywhere was the Torno-Momo car. Having climbed as high as sixth, Baldi plunged headlong into the infield barriers, lucky to sustain only slight concussion and a fractured right ankle. Brake failure, they said.

Jaguar now took up the main running, Nissan seemingly content to learn their way around this 24 Hours business from the acknowledged new masters of the art, the next few hours seeing the other surviving Kidlington Kat establish itself in third. Derek Bell and friends were next, Car #67 going much better since a post-qualifying engine and turbocharger change, their brothers in arms, the Andretti duo, hastily trying to make up ground after having fallen back with a blown tyre then suspension problems.

Joest were going suprisingly well in fifth although already two laps down on the leaders, Old Spice making a remarkable recovery up to sixth having started last after battery failure on the grid when Costas Los overloaded his cool suit. Now, as night descended, their was no reason for such luxuries, the heat of competition replacing falling fahrenheit. They would be around until Sunday lunchtime, no longer.

Night time is the right time at any twice-round-the-clock race, Daytona having half its distance run under floodlights only adding extra emphasis to that part of the equation. Jaguar #60 of Lammers/Jones/Boesel continued to set the pace, the Nissan close enough to move ahead in the rankings at every pitstop, the three hours 'deadline' of its previous longest run passing without drama, its continued good health a source of amazement to most.

*Try as they might the Cobb/Nielsen/ Wallace/Lammers XJR9 could not better second place, eighty-seven seconds in arrears.*

And the scourge of others. Whatever TWR attempted, the Nissan was there. Four hours, five hours, six hours, more, onwards it went into the night and into the unknown, chasing hard. Would nobody rid them of this untroublesome beast?

Brun was climbing up after those early delays for new brakes, Texaco likewise, the Gurney Toyota down and out when overheating cooked its turbo. Mazda were going well, hovering around tenth, as was the Jiffy Lube SE88. It was proving to be one hell of a fight.

And one helluva party too. The infield at Daytona is a lively and crowded place on this, its most special Saturday night of the year. Against a backwash of virtually empty grandstands, a mass of motorhomes and recreational vehicles, Ryder trucks and much more besides, crowd every vantage point, each its own separate empire to the fun. Atop many there sits the remains of a battered settee, its occupants well into the partying mood. It's drinking time at the zoo. Closeby a Winnebago is straddled with something resembling a lookout tower from Fort Apache, a wonderous monument to determination and carpentry skills. Beyond there flies a sign hand-painted on an old bedsheet which explains "We are the people our parents warned us about", while elsewhere a banner says it for one and all with the simple line "Al, we miss you".

The campfires burn bright, the biggest outdoor party in these parts gradually starting to get into gear, the smell of woodsmoke strong in the air, drifting aimlessly across the infield, adding yet another hazard for the race car drivers.

Undeterred by such happenings, having seemingly learned enough, gradually the Nissan started to assert its authority, moving ahead of the Jaguar and opening up a slight advantage. Not slowly but remorselessly, the quartet of heroes taking turns behind its steering wheel were beginning to run the show. Seven hours, eight hours, nine hours, more. . .

Jaguar cracked first. Suddenly and without warning, not long the other side of midnight, Davy Jones brought the top placed XJR9 to a halt on pit road, its engine having given up the ghost, smoke pouring from every orifice. There would be no happy returns for Car #60.

Now they were one-on-one with Nissan, now they had to chase rather than be chased. In those few minutes the whole game had moved on.

As it had for Andretti and Andretti. After an afternoon of woes and an evening of despair which had seen them only climb into the fringes of the top group, they finally called it a day when a faulty brake caliper was added to their list of troubles. There would be no emotional win for 962-HR7, that much was for sure. There would be no 24 Hours success for Mario and Michael.

*. . . closeby a Winnebago is straddled with something resembling a lookout tower from Fort Apache. . . .*

11

That was not to say John could not uphold family honour. He, Bell and Wollek had the Miller car going splendidly, only a lap down on the now second placed Jaguar of Cobb/Nielsen/Wallace and only a further tour behind the ZX-Turbo. Seven laps clear of next best, there seemed nothing to cloud their horizon as Saturday night gave way to Sunday morning.

Except the fog. While the camp fires had kept on burning, added to their smokescreen came this new and more dangerous menace. From high in the skyscraping Winston Tower grandstand opposite pit lane, it could be seen moving inland from the beach like some primaeval force, obliterating everything in its path and settling squarely over the race track.

Cold tyres on a cold track, nobody relished the restart but restart they did. Yet no sooner was the Nissan back up to racing speed than it was pit bound again, any raising of hopes from Jaguar or Busby soon dashed as it went away again after only the routine procedures of fuel and rubber. Fourteen hours down, ten more to go.

But only a couple for 'The Cruise Brothers' and Joest. In a superb display of reliability both of them had done remarkably well, lying fourth and fifth respectively. Then, with the hard work seemingly done, misfortune struck them down almost simultaneously, the Bayside 962 eating a piston for breakfast while Claude Ballot-Lena turned his Blaupunkt version sunny side up without personal injury.

As the fog rolled on in, 200 mph along the back straightaway became reduced to a motorway crawl, so much so that the organisers despatched a pace car in the vain hope it would soon go away. It didn't. Getting thicker by the minute, eventually there was nothing to do but call a halt to proceedings and red flag the race. It was just before two o'clock.

As competitors came to rest in the pitlane, a strange and eerie silence enveloped this place of noise. Under the rules, nobody was allowed to work on their steads, well worn bruised and battered race cars sitting unmolested in a hushed row, the mustard yellow of the Pits Straight arc lamps giving a surreal mellow glow to this lack of proceedings. At first nobody was quite sure what to do, all trying to anticipate how long the stoppage would last, but gradually, one by one, most people drifted off to rest, awaiting the call for a resumption in proceedings whenever the elements deemed to see fit.

Time passed slowly. Hours of it.

The tall electronic score tower down by Turn One gave the first indications of a clear new dawn, its vertical listing of the top placings gradually coming into focus like a beacon of hope. Then, through the last wisps of haze, came the dulcet tones of an official announcement, declaring the restart would be underway in thirty minutes. Gradually, like a sleeping giant awakening from an enforced hibernation, the beat started to pick up, first one, then another engine bursting into life. They had been silent four hours, as near as makes no odds.

Fifteen, sixteen, seventeen and more, eighteen hours passed and still the Nissan drove on, a lap to the good, its pace hindered only slightly by an awkward clutch. But that chink, however slight, gave fresh heart to its pursuers, especially the Busby boys who were gradually making up the early deficit between the trio, Jaguar's cause not helped when they lost a lap with a blown tyre just after sunrise.

Then, minutes before the nineteen hours mark, it happened. The chink became a crack and a big one at that. On lap 444, having lead almost all the way for twelve hours, the Japanese based V6 dropped an exhaust valve. TWR and Busby had finally gotten the break they wanted or, more to the point, Nissan the one they didn't.

Although they tried desperately to continue, their race was all but run, another nine laps and an hour later the smoking machine finally being pushed away into very honourable retirement.

None of the pundits who had predicted its early demise could find solace in the events of Sunday morning, only Jaguar and Busby having reason to be pleased with themselves, their prospects revitalised, and how.

Tom Walkinshaw had once said it takes three years of experience to win a 24 Hours marathon and Nissan had come within an ace of proving that ain't necessarily so. As the Duke of Wellington had commented after the battle of Waterloo: "It was a damn near run thing".

Jaguar versus Porsche, head to head on a Sunday morning, it was the classic encounter. Yet no sooner had Car #61 inherited the lead than it lost it again, the hot morning sun seeing people swimming in the infield's Lake Lloyd as John Andretti went for the jugular, Andy Wallace powerless to thwart his advances. Then Derek Bell took his turn to — literally — drive home the Miller/BFG advantage, as did Wollek, TWR drafting Lammers in to the Castrol car in a last ditch effort to win.

But it was not to be. The Porsche was going like a train, the Jaguar as if a slow coach, only able to narrow but never close the gap which built up between them, the Weissach Wonder not headed over those final vital hours. Later TWR would cite oil temperature problems for their inability to put on more pressure, a malfunctioning oil cooler deemed the culprit.

Porsche cared not. As the Texaco car had done early on Saturday afternoon and the Nissan did for hours on end, the Miller 962 was doing now — leaving the Jaguar trailing in its wake, no black magic by the TWR engineers able to rectify the situation and pull victory from the unwelcome jaws of defeat. Price Cobb's late spin sealed Jaguar's fate: first among losers.

Brun salvaged third, eighteen laps down on the leaders, the Texaco car a further three in arrears. Without those early dramas, both could have played a far more significant role in the final outcome. Mazda were next, their strong run in unfamiliar surroundings surprising many people, the Cherry Hills Tiga eighth and top 'Camel Lights', all the remaining top ten slots taken by all four of Jack Roush's GTO steamroller although not before the Skoal Bandit Camaro had led awhile.

It was, indeed, a memorable victory for the Miller/BF Goodrich team. Not just because it marked the fiftieth by a Typ 962 in IMSA competition or that their winning margin of a shade under 87 seconds was the smallest in the history of what many regard as the toughest 24 Hours race on earth. Nor was it because Jim Busby and his crew had finally laid to rest the spectre which had seen them go four years since their last IMSA laurels.

For John Andretti, it was a first such win, maybe the first of many. Whatever the future holds for him, he was already one up on his more illustrious uncle and cousin despite all their years of trying, collectively and apart.

For Bob Wollek, so often the unlucky man of Le Mans, it was a welcome third victory here. One for his good friend Mauro Baldi who was lying injured in a nearby hospital.

For Derek Bell, it meant a record eighth 24 Hours success, coming as it did after a barren spell of seventeen months out of any winners' circle. He could dedicate it to Al Holbert, the pair inseparable in Daytona and Le Mans legend.

Yet the people for whom this victory meant most were Porsche. Back on the winning trail in 24 Hour marathons once again, the wise men of Stuttgart were looking forward to Le Mans with more than a fair share of renewed optimism.

Last year they had been beaten in the classic encounters by a mere five minutes after forty-eight hours of close fought racing, a blown tyre here and a faulty pump there the small margins between glorious victory and the despair of defeat. Porsche knew above all else that the winners at Daytona were more often than not also the victors at Le Mans — and usually it was themselves. Last season may have been 'The Year of The Cat' but they were determined to ensure 1989 would become known as the season they proved there was life in the old dog yet, the year the biter got bit.

Porsche; Busby; the drivers; they all had something to be very happy about as they took their bows in Victory Lane that day. Winning, like the Miller Lite they drank to celebrate success, tasted sweet and good. The sun was shining and the birds were singing, a strong hint of summer in the air. It was a gloriously golden afternoon.

*Victory lane. Yeh!*

# THE TAMING OF THE SHREWD

**W**HEN THE PAIR of Sauber Mercedes C9/88s swept across the Suzuka finishing line to clinch a glorious one-two victory for the Swiss/German equipe, their win heralded the birth of a whole new era for sports car racing.

Last year FISA had decreed that all rounds of the 1989 World Sports Prototype Championship were to be over a maximum of 480 kms rather than the marathons of ages past. At the stroke of a pen, gone forever were the endurance encounters which could trace their lineage back to the very first world championship race at Sebring in 1953 when Fitch and Walters won for Briggs Cunningham. In between there had been many a classic car and plenty of memorable moments, the likes of D-types at Rheims and Chaparrals at the 'Ring, Pedro Rodriguez in the rain at Brands Hatch and Jacky Ickx doing likewise at Spa, amongst a treasure trove of memories now consigned to the history books.

Nigh-on three hundred races after Sebring'53, never again would a duel be fought out over five or six hours where the ebb and flow of long term tactics and strategy could be taken into account for the final analysis. Le Mans excepted, sports car racing 1989 style would be less like making love with your favourite lady during the course of a long, warm, uninterrupted afternoon than a quick wham, bam, thank you ma'am behind the bike sheds. The end result was still the same, but . . .

Thrash, bash, dash and cash; that's what FISA wanted, something short and sweet. Forget history, said the wise men of Paris, television is what counts, the new shorter format seen as ideal for the all-seeing omnipotent electronic eye. Indeed, there were plans mooted to cut race lengths even further next year as a prequel to the brave new world of 1991 and all the radical changes *that* will bring. Those who supported the new order were unequivocally united in their conviction that such drastic alterations are essential for the long-term survival of the species. Those opposed were divided as to whether it constituted prostitution or rape.

Whatever the pros or cons of it all, the clouds on the horizon when everyone assembled at Suzuka in April were less dogmatic and more down to earth. It was raining.

During the first day of qualifying it rained and rained and rained some more, many teams not bothering even to venture out in the appalling conditions. Quickest of those who did was Derek Bell, still on a high from his Daytona triumph and showing everybody the way round this new WSPC venue in Richard Lloyd's latest adaption of the Porsche theme, its heavily revised aerodynamics making it look more like a Jaguar than a Porsche, more like a Jaguar than a Jaguar.

The TWR Silk Cut outfit themselves also seemed to have an identity crisis. Jaguar knew full well that Mercedes were planning a big onslaught this year but, by their own mountain high standards, seemed at odds to combat the initial forays with their existing XJR9s. Despite having updated the Group C cars mechanically in much the same manner as their IMSA counterparts, almost from the very first time they turned their bigger wheels in practice the parity between them and Sauber which had led to so much close fought racing last season seemed to have vanished, split-seconds a massive gulf when competing at this level. Not this time would there be a string of victories to set them up nicely for 'Le Big One' in June. It would be uphill all the way.

## 'Wham, bam, thank you ma'am'

Yet unofficial photographs had revealed a low-line replacement which nobody was prepared to admit the existance of until it was race ready. Needing to divide themselves between working on the new while not forgetting the old, unfortunately for Jaguar the arrival of the XJR11 was constantly delayed until they were, without doubt, between the devil and the deep blue . . .

. . . although this year it had changed to silver. Mercedes were making no secret of the fact that they were determined to make 1989 the year of the three-pointed star and, as if to underline their determination, the new livery revived memories of days when the so called 'Silver Arrows' of Caracciola and Lang, then Fangio and Moss, blitz-krieged all opposition, feats the modern day heroes were keen to emulate. Nor was it all aesthetics either, new M119 five litre V8s featuring four valves per cylinder allied to their twin turbochargers, seemingly ideal for the task ahead.

Porsche customers were also more upbeat now that the Motronic 1.7 engine management system was readily available to all, thereby revitalising what many people hastily dismissed as redundant hardware. Joest, Kremer and their ilk were keenly experimenting with aerodynamic refinements, as if to emphasise their restored optimism, and were undoubtedly looking forward to the new season considerably more than the previous one. They well remembered that the last Porsche WSPC success had been as long ago as June'87 when Mauro Baldi and Jonathan Palmer won for Lloyd at the Norisring on the same day the 'works' team bowed out from regular competition.

While the factory Porsches had gone in one direction, the Japanese were now headed in the other. Always reluctant to venture beyond their own shores too often, except for Le Mans, new FISA rules wisely stipulated compulsory attendance at all but a single Euro-round of the (supposed) nine-race global schedule. So as the series unfolded Nissan, Toyota and Mazda would all be required to break much new ground if they were to continue their *affaire d'amour* with the French classic. As they signed up for a full term, little did they know what tricks fate had in store for them.

The one selected for Aston Martin cost a cool US$250,000. Their AMR-1 project was already best part of a year behind schedule when a pre-season testing accident wrecked the prototype chassis and forced them to postpone their race debut yet again. And while building a replacement car is an expensive exercise in itself, their load would not be lightened when FISA hit them with the hefty non-attendance fine to add to their troubles. As a way of encouraging new manufacturers to take up the WSPC gauntlet it really was as much a non-starter as the Aston.

Having a much easier time of it, relatively speaking, was Spice Engineering, albeit by dint of their own hard work. Year in and year out for most of the life of the C2 category, Gordon Spice & Co had been the team to beat but now, like their former arch rivals from Ecosse, they were stepping up into the big league.

Spice chose to become the first participants in the new lightweight fuel-free category for normally aspirated engines of up to 3.5 litres which will be *de rigeuer* from 1991 onwards. Then, with their F.1. derivatives, it will be a case of you pays yer money and gets no choice, the

*The France Prototeam Spice C2 was the nearest thing to a threat for Chamberlain, qualifying first in class at Suzuka then finishing second at Dijon.*

wide variety of differing power units currently seen in this form of racing reduced to so much redundant high-speed hardware.

Blessed rather than backed by the Ford Motor Company with the latest versions of the venerable Cosworth V8, the Spice was expected to be particularly at home on the twistier bits later in the season but, alas, Suzuka proved too much too soon for the twin attacks of Ray Bellm/Eliseo Salazar and Wayne Taylor/Thorkild Thyrring when both retired early after a variety of new car problems. A privateer French entry for Henri Pescarolo and Alain Ferte met an even worse fate, failing even to start.

Not that it was all bad news for Spice Eng. They had shown due promise and Jean-Louis Schlesser had casually told 'works' team manager Jeff Hazell that he reckoned the Spice C1 would be the main opposition to his Mercedes over the course of the season. Time would tell.

'Schless' could afford to be magnanimous. After all, he had just won the race. Starting from a suprisingly lowly fourth and partnered by a still hobbling Mauro Baldi, the Frenchman ran away with the event, the only real challenge to Car #61's supremacy coming from the the solus run of team-mate Kenny Acheson. Jochen Mass was supposed to co-drive him but became ill on race day thereby leaving the Ulsterman to battle through nearly three hours unaided after starting from the back of the grid in a car he had not even sat in until that morning! Falling back into line on team orders, Kenny duly finished six seconds behind Schlesser and Baldi. A great effort.

As was that of Bob Wollek and Frank Jelinski aboard Joest's Blaupunkt car. Although forced to cruise home when the fuel gauge reached the red with a few laps still to go, they were the only other car to complete the full distance, even having had the temerity to lead briefly during the sequence of mid-race pit stops. It was a good omen.

Of the other Porsches, theirs was more a tale of what could have been

rather than what was; Derek Bell and Tiff Needell a humble nineteenth for RLR after tyre problems, Brun eighth, Kremer ninth, Tim Lee-Davey nowhere in particular. The Advan/Nova 962 claimed seventh disguised as the Almeras entry, its sister car tenth.

It was quite a good weekend for the locals, all in all, one old Nissan fourth for Suzuki/Hoshino, the other eleventh. Mazda may have had an indifferent time with their IMSA GTP spec- racers but both the new Toyota V8s came good in practice to oust Mercedes from the front row, Barilla/Ogawa finally taking sixth overall after running out of fuel challenging Wollek near the end. Meanwhile, the pole winning Taka-Q version of Geoff Lees and Johnny Dumfries lost time when the Scot executed one of his now customary spins then electrical and fuel maladies slowed progress still further. They had to make do with twentieth.

Three places behind them came the C2 winning Chamberlain Spice Hart of Nick Adams and Fermin Velez. Apparently, all the C2 runners had each received a telephone call from FISA indicating that with an abundance of Japanese C1 entries assured, their participation was not compulsory, they would be excused the trip. As a consequence only four turned up, three competitive prospects and the Roy Baker Racing Tiga.

The France Prototeam Spice headed C2 qualifying but its race lasted only three laps before electric dramas beset it in much the same way as they had sidelined its C1 big sister. Twenty minutes later the Tiga Race Team entry bit the dust with a similar problem thereby leaving Hugh Chamberlain's familiar turbo car safely ahead of RBR.

When the Tiga then stopped for extensive work before struggling on to make a finish, the Buntingford crew enjoyed the most exciting moments of their week. Taking time out after Velez had completed the opening stint, while the race continued around them Adams and 'Le Patron' discussed chapter and verse of the rules regarding minimum lappery required to qualify for points, etc, the fastest man in C2 these past few seasons thereafter destined to cruise the afternoon away but still beating RBR by over fifty miles. Easy peasy.

Oh, that things could have been so simple for the Jags! Switching from radials to cross-plys during practice was never likely to be a good sign, the team in rubber related problems thereafter, although Jan Lammers was truly heroic when he set third fastest qualifying time ahead of all barring the Toyotas in the car he was sharing with Patrick Tambay. Nielsen and Wallace were twelfth.

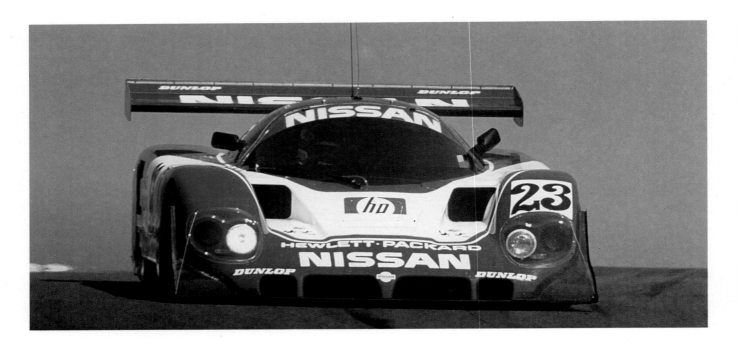

But when it came to the race, the best Jaguar could muster was fifth, John and Andy hampered like so many others by having to stretch their fuel while their team-mates did not make it, falling out of a dissapointing tenth spot on the final lap to complete TWR's most miserable weekend for a very long time. That both cars were the fastest things on the track just before the end counted for little and mattered even less when all was said and done.

And just to add insult to injured pride, more fuel problems meant Lammers was again left to walk home on the last lap at Dijon six weeks later.

Another new WSPC venue, this great drivers' track is probably best remembered for that wheels-within-wheels epic battle between Gilles Villeneuve and Rene Arnoux back in 1979. It certainly would not be forgotten for its poor pitlane and other mediocre facilities ten years later.

Gone was the rain which had dampened the early going in Japan, replaced instead by the warmest May for many a decade, the sunshine bringing with it much which had not been seen in the Orient, notably with regards to the C2 runners and riders.

Also making a low-key *entrée* were Aston Martin. Fearful of another swingeing FISA fine, if truth be told it was still too early for the Newport Pagnell Flyer to be given its wings, a lack of testing reflected in its grid position of twenty-fourth, six places behind the C2 pole. One leading team member was heard to comment as to how their progress could be measured in as much as after the first day here they were 'f***ing awful' while the next simply 'bloody awful'. That Brian Redman and David Leslie managed to get it to the finish, seventeenth, would probably have been termed as a 'bloody miracle'...

Also new was the purposeful looking Nissan, the Lola chassised R89V finally

consigning their old March-based item to the scrap heap not before time. Sixth in qualifying, a splendid showing by Mark Blundell and F.1. refugee Julian Bailey was thwarted by a propensity to pop windscreens as the car bounded over the undulating track, two being lost en route to fifteenth after having earlier been a fighting fourth.

Splitting them at the end was the second C2 car, the Coppelli/Thuner Prototeam Spice having to give best to Adams and Velez again, Chamberlain's duo now in a new Spice Cosworth DFL. Richard Piper's PC/Texas ex-works SE88 was third ahead of Don and James Shead in their McNeil-run example. Andrettis they aren't, but it was still a fine result for a father and son combo who were marking their WSPC debut by putting many a seasoned campaiger in the shade. That is if anybody could find some as the sun continued to swelter!

Bruno Giacomelli and George Fouche were eighteenth in their new composite Kremer 962C-K6 while the best a trio of Brunmobiles could manage was ninth, just ahead of the Mazda and Adams/ Velez. Tim Lee-Davey was nowhere in particular.

The final results actually show TLD to be twenty-fifth and last. Two years ago, armed with his calamitous Tiga Turbo, he had stated as to how all he wanted to do was beat the best C2 Spices, the rest presuming to follow. Slipping three places back from his Suzuka result, you had to wonder how anybody could buy a Porsche and *STILL* have so many problems . . .

As for the C1 versions of his earlier attentions, both had qualified in the top ten then run with the main pack early on before succumbing to various inconveniences, Bellm and new boy Costas Los finally making it into fourteenth while the Taylor/Thyrring twins went out with a broken exhaust primary.

France Prototeam upheld Spice C1

*Same colours, different concepts. Nissan and Aston Martin debuted at Dijon, both making the finish after various dramas.*

honours with a hard won eighth, courtesy of Henri 'Pepsi Cola' and Alain Ferte, while Gallic pride was further enhanced by Ricci/'Ballot' claiming seventh for Joest and Cougar following up fourteenth in Suzuka with an excellent sixth on home soil. Yves Courage's popular little team took the flag just behind the Lloyd 962GTi which may have improved on fifth if it had not required extra stops to fix a door which repeatedly unlatched itself and Lees/Dumfries – reverting to the old car for this one-off race – finished fourth after again starting from the front row. Yet for La Belle France the best was still to come . . .

Up at the sharp end it was another powerful showing by the Saubers but they were unable to make their Michelins work as well as the Goodyears on the char-broiled track and as a consequence could not better second spot for Jean-Louis and Jochen with their team-mates a fraction back in third. Heading them home by half a lap came Jelinski and Wollek in their Akron-shod 962, the aptly dubbed 'Brilliant Bob' from nearby Strasbourg on a roll which had already this season netted him the laurels at Daytona and West Palm Beach plus the opening two German SuperCup rounds, firstly at the Nurburgring then an away fixture on the windswept plains of Silverstone.

Traditionally the Northants track had held the final WSPC race prior to Le Mans, TWR winning each of the last three years before going on to tackle the 24 Hours classic. Not this time. Jaguar won neither the abbreviated Silverstone encounter – a dramatic late entry scratched when the XJR11 was still not race ready – nor the last WSPC hurrah at Dijon.

Stung by their loss of face in Japan, Kidlington had turned up in the Bourgogne keen to make amends. Alas it was not to be. Featuring revised coachwork with the low engine cowl and side ducting very similar to that on view at Daytona three months earlier, Wallace ignored a tyre temperature warning light and ended up spinning into instant retirement when the right rear Dunlop called his bluff just after half distance. He was sixth at the time.

And then as the laps wound down, Dumfries was chasing the Lammers/Tambay #1 car only to have his work done for him when the Jag's fuel pump went on strike less than a mile from home.

Last year at Silverstone, Jan had seen a certain top three placing disappear when his then team-mate Dumfries had suffered fuel pump failure just before the finish. Coincidence or destiny, then as now Lammers was out of luck and would go off to Le Mans pointless. Then

he had come back a winner. Would history make it a win-double for the Dutchman?

The ACO, organisers of The Great Race, tried to sum up a maelstrom of mixed emotions with their post-Dijon press bulletin which did not need much by way of translation when remarking how 'once again Jaguar were beaten, all hopes of their carrying off the WSPC title already virtually gone. Now the Walkinshaw team must win at Le Mans to save its season'.

TWR would have begged to differ that 1989 had already come down to the make or break of a single event yet there were plenty of others – Sauber, Porsche, the Japanese et al – preparing to spoil the anniversary party for them, everyone only too aware that Le Mans is special, Le Mans is different. For sure, the Silk Cats would be a far tougher proposition over *Les Vingt-Quatre Heures* than they had been at either Suzuka or Dijon.

Yet the equally divided score between Stuttgart's finest symbolised this to be the most open Le Mans for years, the likes of Nissan and Toyota full of eastern promise. Adding the hoped-for dash of Aston Martin and the bravado of Courage with more than a hint of Spice and it was all looking good as the Sarthois High Holy Days fast approached.

Anything could happen and probably would.

# AS YOU LIKE IT

"DO YOU KNOW . . . ? Have you heard . . . ?". The telephone lines were abuzz with rumour and speculation.

It was in those last few days before the Silverstone SuperCup race – a week prior to Dijon's second round of the WSPC and less than a month before the annual Le Mans extravaganza – when news started to filter through that all was not well between FISA and the Automobile Club de l'Ouest.

When FISA decided to take more control of the World Sports Prototype Championship as from this year, they wanted to include certain provisos into their modus operandi. Amongst the organising aspects to come directly under the control of the Parisians were to be those of race timekeeping and also the much more vexed question of television rights.

Yet whereas many of the tracks seemed only too pleased to hand over such control to FISA in order to guarantee their inclusion in the championship, the ACO were not. They knew, as everybody else did, that their race was worth all of the six or seven or eight other WSPC rounds put together, however many there would eventually be. In the idiom of the day, the ACO has 'clout'.

Longines/Olivetti were the FISA choice for timekeepers, the Geneva based FOCA Television nominated to beam coverage to an awaiting world. The ACO, for their part, were quite happy to retain Oce as their official timekeepers and were reluctant to break an existing contract with TF1 apropos television rights to what is, arguably, the world's most famous motor race. It seemed as if, at last and somewhat inevitably, the irresistible force had met the immovable object.

Throughout the early months of the year reports appeared of the divide between them, FISA thrusting and the ACO parrying, a battle of wills raging behind almost closed doors. Finally, so everybody thought at the end of March, came news that the dispute had been settled, the ACO getting much of their own way but with a proviso to attend fresh talks soon after this year's event so as to sort out the rules of engagement for next season. With the main topic of discussion inevitably to be regarding the magic box and FOCA Television based in the Swiss town, it would undoubtably become the WSPC equivelent of the Geneva Convention. Rusty bayonets at dawn?

But that was all for the future, for now FISA issued a bulletin indicating that TF1 would retain the rights of France and Japan, FOCA getting the rest. Alas, it appears that nobody had not asked the French channel what they thought of it so far . . .

As a consequence, the bonhomie lasted only six weeks, the whole matter erupting once again in mid May thereby making the Silverstone paddock grapevine more exciting than any race seen there that SuperCup weekend. TF1, it was soon revealed, wanted FF2,000,000 in compensation for lost revenues, something FISA were unwilling to pay.

Rumour and counter-rumour; plot and counter-plot; the air was rife with more differing opinions as to what would happen than at a tea-leaf readers' convention. Some suggested there would not be a race at all this year, others of the opinion that it would go ahead this time but next year was in jeopardy. Rumour and counter-rumour, plot and counter-plot.

Yet a week is a long time in motor racing politics, and as everyone assembled at Dijon came news of a settlement, an official statement issued on behalf of both parties advising that "taking into account the personality, specific nature and heritage of the Le Mans competition, it was decided by mutual agreement that it is in the interests of the event to remain outside the World Championship for 1989". Bland and blunt, leaving out more than it said, the upshot of it was that the WSPC crown had lost its most precious jewel.

Putting on a brave and united face in public, having obviously agreed only to differ, the ACO and FISA appeared to be at one – but not everybody was pleased with the way things had turned out, the Japanese teams smarting that they had been lured into doing the whole

WSPC season so as to gain access to Le Mans only to discover that now it was not necessary. They were not amused, although history may yet record that by making them come more out in the open than before, it will be the best thing that can ever have happened to them. Time will tell.

As it will regarding the future status of the Le Mans 24 Hours and what FISA will do to help it return to the umbrella of the World Sports Prototype Championship for next year and beyond. If the ACO wants it to return, that is, their opposition to the 3.5 litre rules of 1991 already well known.

What was clear, though, was that teams not originally eligible for entry into this year's race by dint of not being fully paid up members of the regular WSPC circus, teams like WM Peugeot and ADA Engineering, were suddenly packing their bags and heading for La Sarthe, in with a chance they thought would never come. And with none of the main contenders pulling out despite the loss of championship status, it effectively made for an even better entry list than ever.

So the cry went up: "To hell with the politics, let's get on with the racing!". And they surely would. This time . . .

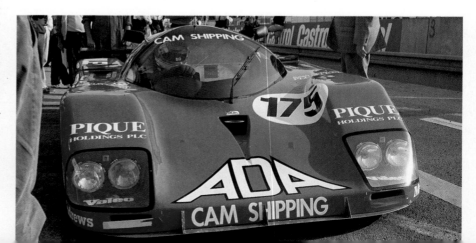

# GREAT EXPECTATIONS

FIRST CAME THE SOUND. Then came the vision.

Like a silver bullet fired from a magic gun, the Sauber Mercedes barrelled down the straight and around the corner and away. Jean-Louis Schlesser was on a quick one.

A sports car racing superstar, a hero of all France, with the awesome Mulsanne now behind him, Indianapolis and Arnage were next, the thunderous five litre turbocharged V8 preceded by its own wall of sound, something of a nature not heard since Joshua fought the Battle of Jericho. Left into one, right around the other, up through the gearbox and gone, chasing that bright orange orb which now hung low in the evening sky.

Accelerating hard, the Porsche Curves beckoned, sweeping one way then the other, it was down through the 'box and hard on the brakes, through the Virage Ford and off into the sunset.

Jean-Louis Schlesser was on a very quick one: he stopped the clocks at 3m15.04s. A year and a day, almost to the minute, since a flailing tyre had so cruelly ripped Peter Sauber's ambitions to shreds, 'Schless' had finally put the car he would share with former F.1. ace Jean-Pierre Jabouille and tin-top exponent Alain Cudini beyond the realms of all others and with it expunged the nightmare of '88.

And just to drive home the message in the best possible way came Mauro Baldi, teamed with Kenny Acheson and Gianfranco Brancatelli, to make it a glorious one-two for the Three Pointed Star. Oh, what joy. Oh, what relief . . .

Yet all was not well with the Suisse-Allemagne equipe, their #63 car of Jochen Mass, Manuel Reuter and Stanley Dickens down at eleventh having suffered a variety of gearbox problems which cast doubts over the whole Sauber challenge. Indeed, the transmissions were deemed to be the weak link in an otherwise impressive package of speed and reliability and as none of the Mercedes engined devices had *EVER* run beyond half distance at Le Mans before in four years of trying, there were many who doubted their ability to do so this time – including some very close to the centre of the Hinwil/Stuttgart action. Fast but fragile, that was the general consensus of opinion . . .

Just like the Nissans at Daytona. Coincidentally, the slowest Sauber lined up immediately alongside the fastest Nissan on Row Six, the Japanese team not willing to attempt any Qualifying heroics at La Sarthe despite having the Daytona front running – and Sebring winning – trio of Geoff Brabham, Arie Luyendyk and Chip Robinson on the payroll. Fifteenth after all manner of woes caused mainly by a broken water pipe, top in-house honours, twelfth, finally went to Martin Donnelly who was a shade quicker than Julian Bailey in the car they would share with Mark Blundell, all three new to the race. The car crewed by Hasemi, Hoshino and Toshio Suzuki quietly slid into nineteenth, nobody expecting too many fireworks from #23.

Toyota were reckoning on a few of their own – and got less than they bargained for. At scrutineering two days earlier, team leader Geoff Lees had put aside both his English reserve and any Japanese inscrutability which had come his way over the years while driving the Orient expresses, to state that he was out to get pole position and would be "very disappointed" if the prize was denied him. He didn't and he was.

As with everyone else, Toyota's main shot at the top slot had to be deferred until the second day of Qualifying after a very heavy downpour part way through Wednesday's early session had sent everyone scampering for cover, washing away any chance of hot times. Now with Lees determined to secure the first Japanese pole at Le Mans, for a long time he held it with a fine 3m15.51s only to be denied his moment of glory when disqualified for having used a T-car, Schlesser's subsequent bettering of his efforts only adding insult to injured pride. Geoff had been fast but now he was furious, this silly *faux pas* a repeat of something which happened at Mount Fuji three years ago. Relegated to seventeenth on the grid, it was poor reward for such a brave effort.

Aboard the Taka-Q 89CV with the expatriate Midlander on race day would be former Jaguar colleagues John Watson – making his first outing of the season – and Johnny Dumfries, the Scottish earl commenting drily how the difference between driving for the Jags and the Japs was that the latter pay more money! Whatever the truth of it, to be sure Geoff Lees would have given a royal ransom to have had his time stand.

Two more Toyotas, another of the new omnipotent V8s and the old straight-four seen at Dijon, would share Row Thirteen between them. Unlucky thirteen. It was all starting to go ominously wrong for the men from Team Tom's.

Tom's team were fairing much better, this despite the fact of their week having gotten off to the most horrendous of starts when a young engineer, Steve Harding, was killed in a road accident on Tuesday, his death putting a pall of despair over the Walkinshaw enclave, team members closing ranks in their despondency. "We are just going through the motions" said one of his colleagues with meaning. You really could feel for them.

But the show must go an and go on it did. With the Saubers hogging the headlines up front, third on the grid came Jan Lammers, the TWR team leader commenting as to how the car felt

**JEAN-LOUIS SCHLESSER** (Sauber #62): "The pole position lap was good but not very clear. I had a few problems with traffic but imagine others had them too. On my quick lap I came across another car in the Kink and lost one thousand revs, about two seconds, but knew it was still good enough for pole position. That is why I came in straight away – but I also know it could have been better.

"I think I can win it otherwise I would not come here. I'd be a television commentator!"

**GEOFF LEES** (Toyota #37): "I shall be very disappointed if we are not on pole position. The performance will also be pretty good in the race and I think we can finish in the first three.

"One thing you have to remember is that our car is not built by Lola or anybody else but by Toyota. It is our own car. We have built everything. This is the first time we have done it and straight away it is competitive."

**JOHN WATSON** (Toyota #37): "I'm sure the first half of the race will be very quick, a lot quicker than last year. Then, with the Jaguar winning from the front as it did, it finally dispelled the myth about this being a 24 Hours race. It is a sprint which lasts for 24 hours."

**GEOFF BRABHAM** (Nissan #25): "The first time I ever saw the place was yesterday, Tuesday. It really is impressive. The race track is definitely fast and challenging so it will be a very interesting race to do. The fact that my brother is here (with a Schuppan Porsche) adds a little bit more excitement to it, a race within a race.

**CHIP ROBINSON** (Nissan #25): "Twenty-four hour races are not my favourite but it is not as if I hate them like some guys do. They keep asking themselves why they keep coming back, I know why I come back – it's because I want to win! But if they left the schedule it is not as if I'd be upset about that either. . ."

*A rose amongst the thorns. Lyn St.James poses at scrutineering surrounded by teammates Spice, Bellm, Harvey, Taylor and Thyrring plus a selection the crew.*

*Various drivers tried the Sauber T-car. . .*

*. . . but it was Jean-Louis Schlesser who notched pole position, much to the obvious pleasure of compatriots Tambay, Ricci, Pescarolo and Raphanel.*

as good as last year's. He obviously hoped for the result to stand too. Fourth was Davy Jones in another of the purple predators. Race prospects were looking good for TWR Jaguar.

Although the Kidlington equipe had not had the best of it so far this season, fifth at Suzuka not much to show for a lot of effort, nobody was underestimating their potential when it came to The Great Race despite the entourage being downscaled from last term. Instead of five cars there were but four, instead of imported Indycar megastars there were more down-to-earth talents, the Ferte brothers, Alain and Michel, from just up *la rue* at Falaise – birthplace of William the Conqueror – leading the way. Neither of them had ever raced a Jaguar before, and nor had Andrew Gilbert-Scott, the young F3000 racer revelling in his chance to emulate last year's British new boy Andy Wallace and win first time out at Le Mans. Teamed with Lammers and Patrick Tambay such a thing was distinctly possible.

The line up of drivers – which included all the Daytona crew save for Martin Donnelly and Raul Boesel – was completed by Eliseo Salazar and Jeff Kline, a 45-years old Le Mans rookie who had made such a hit with his performance at The Big D four months earlier, thereby putting himself firmly in the ring for a slug at the heavyweight title. Salazar, for his part, preferred to avoid any references to boxing, still unable to play down the fact his most famous role to date was as Nelson Piquet's punchbag at Hockenhein in 1982.

The other two XJRs locked in to sixth and eighth, all four in the top six during Saturday's morning warm-up. A full ten miles an hour faster down Mulsanne than last year without the benefit of being able to wind up boost knobs like virtually all of their rivals, it was indication enough that although the cars looked much the same as before things had not been idle at the House of Walkinshaw and everyone there was determined to hold on to the crown so

spectacularly won twelve months ago.

The crown won from Porsche. Still on a high from Daytona and Dijon, the 'other' Stuttgart manufacturer really fancied their chances hereabouts, factory team or no factory team.

"It is an eighty per cent works car" said Hans Stuck in that lovely lilting accent of his, when questioned about the pink Blaupunkt/Italya 962, the presence of Porsche factory sage Norbert Singer alongside team owner Reinhold Joest reiterating the point, if such a thing was necessary. Everywhere you looked their were Weissach personnel 'on holiday'; top engineers assigned not only to Joest but also Kremer, Schuppan and Brun – competitions chief Peter Falk and engine man Harald Schmidt circulating between all those who used the company's famous flat-six power plant. Gone may have been the official 'works' entries but the Porsche factory was at Le Mans in quite some force, of that there could be no doubt. Joest or Kremer, Schuppan, Brun or whoever; a win by any of these by any name would still be a win for Porsche.

Stuck was paired with Bob Wollek, a straw poll around the paddock showing the dynamic duo to be most people's favourites for victory, an un-retired 'John Winter' pencilled in to help them if necessary. And on Wednesday it looked as if they might need all the help they could get when their special high-boost Qualifying engine let go on 'Brilliant Bob' just as he was getting into his stride, the blushing pink #9 pushed ignominiously away to the paddock for a replacement.

Restored to good health the following evening, nevertheless the new unit was in race-spec and although sent out on Goodyear's stickiest rubber, Hans was strictly limited to race boost when he scorched round to grab fifth place on the grid – despite heavy traffic and the tyres losing their grip after only half a lap. It was a stunning performance typical of both man and machine, an ominous sign.

And not one lost on the ever ebullient

Hanschen : "I have been on pole position twice in the last four years but did not win whereas on the two occasions in between where I have not started from pole I won the race. Maybe it is a good omen for us!". And a bad one for everybody else.

Neither Henri Pescarolo (a four-times winner) or Claude Ballot-Lena have ever gotten a pole position at La Sarthe despite this being the twenty-third race for both men. Partnered together for the first time, Jean-Louis Ricci made up the trio who would start back in an unrepresentative thirty-fourth after gearbox problems spoilt their Qualifying efforts.

Not last and not least for Joest came the latest rendition of their famous Number #7, 'Winter' transferring over to partner Frank Jelinski and Pierre-Henri Raphanel onto the seventh row, the latter being – with Mazda man Volker Weidler – the only 1989 Grand Prix pilote on show, if that is what you can call someone who drives the second Coloni . . .

JEFF KLINE (Jaguar #3): "It is very difficult for a newcomer to learn the track as you only see every corner once every 3 minutes. Going down Mulsanne in an absolute rush is really incredible, the car accelerating all the way, doing about 240 mph by the end. It's a really interesting experience to go that fast, a no-brainer until you get to the Kink. If you're going to go out at 220 you might as well do it at 240 . . ."

DAMON HILL (Porsche #15): "I spoke to Richard Lloyd about a month ago and he said he did not think there would be a chance as they were only running one car. But then he 'phoned me up last week to say they were taking two and to come up to Silverstone for a few laps. I did about four.

"When my Dad won, I can remember it being broadcast on the radio and I did not even know he was doing it! I was more interested in what I was doing at the time. I knew he was a racing driver but that was all. It's good that he won it. Me? It's all about being there at the finish. . ."

WILL HOY (Porsche #33): I used to go down the straight looking in the C2 mirrors for the C1s to go past. Now I am in a C1 Porsche, it's nice to pass more people than being passed! When I did my qualifying stint there were a couple of times down Mulsanne when I really did not know which way the C2s were going to go. You see a car wandering a bit, you know he has not been looking in his mirrors for a few seconds. . ."

CHRIS HODGETTS (Mazda #201): "I only signed the contract to drive on Wednesday morning and have only done eleven laps in practice; never having sat in the car until that evening. In the night, in the fog, pebbles all over the circuit. And wet. A real baptism of fire!"

WAYNE TAYLOR (Spice #22): "I was on dry tyres and had just gotten down to the end of the Mulsanne when the heavens opened up. So I radioed I was coming in.

"I got to the Porsche Curves, cruising along in second gear, and the Lloyd car came flying past me. I thought he must be on wets but the next thing I knew he was spinning in front of me. I thought I was going to T-bone it so spun to avoid him, just touching the back of the barrier. Facing the oncoming traffic, I was half out of the car when it caught my eye that the Mazda was coming for me. It looked as if it was going to land on the windscreen! So I jumped back in and tried to get myself up in the cockpit and it hit me head on. I was staring at the underneath of it as it flew over the top! It wasn't his fault, he just aquaplaned. It was not as if he was going that fast. I just happened to be there . . ."

Oscar Larrauri was in F.1. last year, partnering Stefano Modena in the un-loved Brun mobile chicane. Now back concentrating on sports cars, 'Popi' pushed the #17 Repsol car into a surprising seventh spot – and quickest during Saturday's warm up – to become one of the dark horses of the race, his only complaint being that co-drivers Jesus Pareja and Walter Brun were not up to his speed and likely to slow his progress. Not that he complained too much. You wouldn't, would you, if one of your partners was named Jesus and the other is the guy who pays your wages . . .

Two slots further back, Sarel 'Super Van' der Merwe took Brun's From-A version by the scruff of its gaudy yellow neck to clinch ninth while fellow South African George Fouche rounded off the top ten in the equally colourful Leyton House 962 for the brothers Kremer, their Kenwood entry fourteenth.

Mazda #202 grabbed sixteenth just behind the 'American' Nissan, the other two of their IMSA GTP entries back in the pack. A full eight seconds faster than last year thanks to a new variable injection system, there were those who seriously reckoned the screaming wonders could do as well if not better than their fifth place at Daytona in February for Takashi Yorino, Elliott Forbes-Robinson and Yoshini Katayama. Not that Yoshini-san would be around to help his team-mates to any possible glories on this occasion having bitten off more than he could chew and ended up in hospital with food poisoning rather than at Le Mans with a race to run.

Chris Hodgetts, helmet in hand, was in the right place at the right time to take advantage of this unexpected opportunity, signing up on Wednesday morning and having completed less than a dozen laps in the car by the time Qualifying finished.

#202 had benefitted by being the only one of the three Mazdas not to suffer major practice dramas, the most serious being an accident which befell Marc Duez on Wednesday evening. Caught out in that oh-so-sudden downpour, he had slid up into and over a stationary Wayne Taylor who had, seconds earlier, gone off in the Spice C1 while trying to avoid Tiff Needell's gyrating RLR Porsche. The orange and green Mazda machine was very heavily damaged, it's driver shaken but not stirred.

Tiff was unscathed but as for Wayne, the 'former' South African was lucky to get away with a badly bruised arm.

His SE89C did not get off so lightly, its repairs taking all the next day with the right-front chassis corner having to be flown in from England then grafted on. Taylor, Thorkild Thyrring and Tim Harvey were simply relieved to be in the race despite being only in thirty-seventh starting slot five places down on team-patrons Ray Bellm and Gordon Spice who were joined for the occasion by

*Oscar Larrauri contemplates seventh in Qualifying, less than half a second shy of 'Stucky'. An excellent effort.*

American lady racer Lyn St. James.

Tiff – or 'Terrific Tiff' as he had recently decided he wanted to be known – had damaged the underside of his PCGB/Cabin Porsche during his attempts at improvised landscaping, but this was not the root cause of problems in Richard Lloyd's well fancied team. The cars – this one also being run for Derek Bell and James Weaver with the other (a bare tub only a week before) handled by David Hobbs, Steven Andskar and Damon Hill – were about thirty miles-per-hour too slow down Mulsanne. Their status as possible winners was fast disappearing with their inability to overcome the difficulties.

"We are about six seconds too slow" said a decidedly morose Derek Bell on Friday evening, his post-Qualifying mood no better than it had been at Daytona. "We are working on it but it's all a bit late in the day now." For the five times winner things were going to get a lot worse before they got better. Then worse again.

Not that all was doom and gloom chez Lloyd, young Damon Hill, son of the 1972 winner, only too pleased to have been given such an opportunity knowing how time served with the same Silverstone equipe had levered open so many doors for Martin Donnelly. A famous name is one thing but drives and results are what gets you noticed in this game and Hill was determined to be as upwardly mobile as the Ulsterman.

The PCGB/Cabin #14 would start from twenty-second, the black PCGB/Raika #15 version twenty-fourth. Decidedly underwhelming.

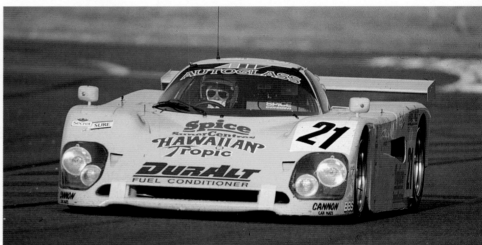

*Meanwhile, Jan Lammers was again top gun for Jaguar, third on the grid and a full five seconds quicker than last year.*

*After having the dubious honour of viewing the underside of a wet Mazda at speed, Wayne Taylor also tried out Spice #21.*

Sandwiched between them on the grid came the Takefuji Schuppan 962 of coming-men Will Hoy, Jean Alesi and Dominic Dobson. Unfortunately all sorts of problems regarding brakes and aerodynamics prevented the Number #33 car from figuring more strongly in the 'Essais'.

Their sister car did much better. Handled by Vern Schuppan himself, Eje Elgh and new recruit Gary Brabham – famous sons of famous fathers a feature of this year's classic – the blue Omron ex-Andretti car was comfortably into the top half dozen early in Qualifying before dropping back to concentrate on a good race set-up, finally settling for eighteenth. Unable to contain their enthusiasm for their prospects for the race, team members were confident that if anybody could upset the form book it could well be them.

Three more 962s filled the middle of the grid; one Alpha, a second Repsol and one Hydro Aluminium example, all courtesy of Brun Motorsport. Their general lack of pace might possibly have been something to do with the fact that they were already pre-sold to either private collectors or museums.

Another three Porsches filled the bottom half of the grid. Les freres Almeras had upped their own particular ante-after years of running lesser Porsches while for Obermaier a smiling Pierre Yver explained that having come second here two years ago 'Old Faithful' would again be run in its customary 'soto voce' mode in an endeavour for more success. "We intend to go one better" said the man from La Manche, the laughter in his voice more in hope than expectation.

Not so happy was Tim Lee-Davey. Poor Tim! His still (almost) new machine looked somewhat second-hand when it arrived – and decidedly more so after Nipponese renta-driver Katsunori Iketani threw it into the kitty-litter early in the week, TLD's resourcefulness once again being stretched to the limit. Sharing with Tom Dodd-Noble, forty-fourth was a long way to come back from.

Yves Courage, local boy made good, had come back from a fine third spot in 1987 to have his dreams crushed and go up in smoke twelve months later, one of his Cougar Porsches destroyed in a fearful accident, the other consumed by a pitlane fire. Now, with a matched pair of C22 LMs driven circumspectly throughout by the likes of Pascal Fabre and Bernard de Dryver, he hoped to build on a fine sixth place at Dijon, an old March Nissan also entered under the Courage banner but run separately by Tom Hanawa's LMC team.

One place behind the March, forty-first, came the second Aston Martin, this latest example of the AMR-1 only being finished off in time for the second session of Wednesday's events. Driven by team boss Ray Mallock with David Leslie and David Sears, they were eight places down on the example which had debuted at Dijon and was now in the care of Brian Redman / Costas Los / Michael Roe. All were diplomatically complimentary about the story so far despite both cars being noticably off the pace along Mulsanne due to an apparent over abundance of downforce.

Whatever the limitations of their challenge it was good to see – and hear – such a famous name back at Le Mans with a fully fledged 'works' effort for the first time since their historic win exactly thirty years ago, Prince Michael of Kent amongst those who stopped by to give the team some morale support. For sure, everyone involved in the project knew there would be no such glories on this occasion, the patriotic red-white-and-blue noise box only coveting a chance to finish. Short of miles, bereft of a designer – pen man Max Bostrom having departed the scene 'by mutual agreement' an ill-timed two weeks earlier – the scent was not of victory, the signs more akin to 'Running In, Please Pass'. Maybe that is why they have such big rear view mirrors . . .

RAY MALLOCK (Aston Martin #18/19): "I don't know why it should appear to be big, maybe it is the colour scheme or it could be the engine noise which makes it sound like a big brute!"

While the Astons were aiming for a new life in the fast lane, WM Secateva were heading in the opposite direction, the 'very French' little team from just east of Paris, soon to be disbanded, their being no place in tomorrow's world for adventurers only wishing an occasional outing. Indeed, they would not have been here this time save for the A C O's late withdrawal from the title chase, thereby opening the entry list to a greater and more varied clientele.

For more than a decade this happy band had provided the race with much spectacle and colour even if not a lot by way of positive results, their most abiding postscript surely to be that 400 kph down Mulsanne last year. Enthusiastic to the point of mania, WM epitomised the essence of those days when little guys could take on the big guns in this most cosmopolitan of arenas, the chance of glory always present, the opportunities to succeed invariably proving elusive. This would be their last hurrah.

24

*WM #51 spun out, flamed out and finally bowed out. What a way to go!*

*Hello Leicester Square. Chamberlain were unable to make it three Le Mans C2 poles in succession but were still the car to beat. Until 9 o'clock Sunday morning. that is. . .*

Not that the WM saga was likely to just quietly fade away, such a thing not being their style. Partway through Thursday's sessions Phillipe Gache had a turbo blow on the run down towards Indianapolis, the subsequent conflagration engulfing his #51 car – which had qualified encouragingly in midfield – almost immediately. Trapped inside for what seemed to be an age, the F3000 man was fortunate to escape unharmed.

What you lose on the swings you gain on the roundabouts; and in the helter skelter world of the jolly green giants what was bad for WM #51 became an absolute bonus for WM #52. The team had been going through Peugeot V6s as if there was no tomorrow (for sure there would be no next week) to the point where there was only one race engine available for the two cars. The demise of #51 ensured its destiny and a start for Gache (who transferred his allegiance but not his luck), J-D Raulet and Pascal Pessiot one spot behind Lee-Davey.

Another for whom the fire bell tolled was the Mussato Lancia, the much rebuilt and revised cantankerous old warhorse finally ending all its hopes of any Italian brio making the grid when a turbocharger blew asunder on Thursday evening taking parts of the Ferrari made crankcase with it, clouding the pits and much of Northern France in a fogbank of steam and disappointment. Arreverderci, Roma.

Hello, Leicester Square. Hugh Chamberlain had once been a policeman in nearby Kentish Town but he was powerless to arrest the progress of Jean-Philippe Grand's new Graff Spice Cosworth as it scorched around in 3m38.70s to clinch the C2 pole with thirty-eighth overall.

Hugh's own flying squad had taken the category's top slot on each of the last two years courtesy of some stunning lappery by Nick Adams but this time it was not to be, French customs officials delaying the Buntingford team's special qualifying unit sufficiently long enough to ensure Gallic honour was upheld. Adjusting their losses accordingly, it was even left to Nick's diminuitive Spanish partner, the 1987 C2 co-champion Fermin Velez, to do best for the Brits three seconds and four places further back in the car they were to share with Gigi Taverna, the similar Lombardi entry next up.

*Arriverderci Roma. A blown turbocharger foiled the attempts of Coppelli and Scapini to qualify the Lancia.*

In fact C2 was all about Spice, Spice and almost nothing but Spice, the France Prototeam example fourth followed closely by the second Chamberlain entry – this one featuring their familiar 1800cc of Hart turbo – for John Hotchkis' senior and junior along with Richard Jones who again turned up without a drive booked only to find himself drafted into the team when the contracted American pilot had difficulties. Last year, Bobby Ore was too big, this time Les Delano absent without leave after missing his Concorde connection. One man's disappointment is another man's unexpected opportunity.

Along with the Hart came the dream, the Curtain Dream Spice of powerboater Don Shead partnering fellow rookies Ross Hyett and Robbie Sterling. Doing

a good job under John McNeil's guidance, theirs was a careful and methodical approach interrupted only by the WM's rather irritating habit of firing pieces of exploding Peugeot V6 at them. Nobody would bet against Mako having proper hardware for the trophy cabinet come Sunday afternoon.

Last but not least of the Spices was GPM at eighth in class, fiftieth overall, the Dianetique device attracting all sorts of disasters to itself including a clash of more than just temperaments between Dudley Wood and the Blaupunkt Porsche of perfume heir Ricci on Thursday evening, neither coming off smelling of roses. Things could only improve.

One spot ahead of GPM was the Cougar Porsche of veteran new owner Philippe Farjon, Shunji Kasuya and

rally man Jean-Claude Andruet. Detuned from the car which finished third overall only two years ago, its much anticipated sling-shot at C2 pole never materialised.

Nor did the anticipated challenge from ADA. Three places further back surrounded by a trio of toothless Tigas, the West Londoners looked a long way off adding to their hard won second place last year after another drama filled practice ruined their progress. Next in line, recalcitrant in extremis, the Speedy Argo seemed fit only to be sued for misrepresentation . . .

And last of all – along with the barbequed Lancia – came a quartet of ALDs, none of these longtime stalwart supporters of all things Sarthois able to muster sufficient *vitesse* between them to have gotten even one car in amongst the qualifiers, the race seeming destined to start without them.

Yet luck was on their side. WM were unable to repair their charred wreck and did not have an engine for it even if they could, their sole surviving race unit having already been transferred to its sister machine. As a consequence grid position twenty-one was vacated moving everybody up a notch, the ALD Cosworth which had easily outrun its three BMW powered cousins if nothing else, slipping happily onto the tail of the queue.

And so it was done, Qualifying over for another year. There had been much to commend it and little to doubt that this would be the 'Clash of the Titans' held over twelve months since that dramatic withdrawal of the Saubers last time around. Mercedes versus Porsche versus Jaguar, it had the makings of a classic.

All three were in with a really good chance of pulling off the prize, the Japanese – 'le peril jeune' according to at least one ACO press release – also likely to put on their strongest showing ever although nobody, deep down, was really expecting them to win. There again nobody had been expecting their Yankee cousins to do so well at Daytona or Sebring either.

To most minds Le Mans '89 would still be a very European affair. Mercedes had arrived here with something to prove and stood the test well. Now would come the race itself, twenty-four hours in which to finally steel their mettle against all-comers, not least near-neighbours Porsche who were eager to show all those who dared write off their efforts that there was life in the 962 yet, the company only having been beaten here once, by less than three minutes, since Group C began back in 1982.

That was last year, by a Jaguar, something the Coventry marque were determined to repeat. Chastened by having gone half a season – both in WSPC and IMSA – without victory, nobody, but nobody, had a greater incentive to win than the guys and gals behind the four Silk Cats who had seen their week shattered by the loss of a colleague yet rallied to perform so well.

While the minds went out to the strong men of Stuttgart, the hearts felt for Kidlington.

Anything could happen and probably would.

*Derek Bell, Britain's ultimate Le Mans hero. Not that he had a lot to smile about this time.*

DEREK BELL (Porsche #14): "I think on Joest's past record they should beat the Jags. I shouldn't do so, but I dismiss Mercedes because although they are going so well they have got to do it for 24 Hours which is a different deal altogether. I think it will take them another year in which to do it. If a Porsche or a Jaguar run faultlessly it will beat the Mercedes. I don't think they can hang it out at that long at that pace – yet – unless they have been bloody good. Nobody else has done it in the history of motor racing. But then the Germans and the Mercs are pretty bright kids . . ."

# THE PURPLE PIMPERNEL

*"They seek him here, they seek him there.
They seek Tom Walkinshaw everywhere.
Is he in heaven? Is he in hell?
That famed and elusive Purple Pimpernel."*

OFF TO Watkins Glen one day; back for a visit to the Royal Agricultural Show the next; be it dinner at the House of Commons or a working continental breakfast; nothing in the Walkinshaw empire moves as fast as 'Major Tom' himself – and that includes a XJR9LM!

Tom Walkinshaw is a hard man to pin down, a hard man full stop. Anyone who had the privelege of seeing him wield 1½ tons of Jaguar XJS muscle car around Brno or Bathurst, Silverstone or Spa knows that if he had been raised on the chewin' tobacco of the Deep South rather than the porridge of Auld Caledonie he would surely have been a NASCAR hero. Instead, he became the toast of European touring cars and now one of sports-prototype's ultimate legends as the man who brought the Coventry Cats leaping back to the very top of world motorsport.

The man with the midas touch; almost everything he seems to do turns to gold. Big race wins by the dozen; championships by the score; double WSPC Teams' and Drivers' titles these past two seasons were crowned with stunning 1988 victories at Daytona then Le Mans.

"Contrary to popular belief, I do not screw every nut and bolt onto the motor cars myself. If I did that I would want walking off!" he says in a brief moment of respite, the burr of his Lothian tongue resonating around the close confines of the TWR motorhome which, for now, with his presence, is the focal point of a burgeoning business empire. Outside there is a race to run, places to go and people to meet, the company's helicopter and LearJet on permanent stand-by. Tom Walkinshaw never got where he is today by sitting still for long.

Maybe he is not in line to take over Jaguar in the same way that Roger Penske is said to be ready to buy General Motors, but with thirty-something companies employing over six hundred people, he is constantly on the move, wheeling and dealing, instructing and consulting. Here, there and everywhere; you could get get the impression that neither his family or his staff know where he is likely to turn up next!

Thomas Dobbie Thomson Walkinshaw first appeared on the scene back in 1946, not far from the Edinburgh base of the legendary Ecurie Ecosse who did so much to make the Jaguar name at Le Mans in the fifties. But he quickly refutes suggestions of their being any particular sentiment towards his forebears in his efforts thirty years later:

"It has never crossed my mind. They did a good job at the time but we are doing something completely different. It is not connected in any way, shape or form. I can remember listening to the Le Mans races on the radio, but Jim Clark lived just down the road from my parents' farm so he, I think, was more of an influence in stimulating motor racing thoughts up there than Ecurie Ecosse."

Nor is his appreciation of their efforts helped by his own unproductive association with the reconstituted team at a critical time in his driving career. The man who is adamant that he has never sat in any of his Group C/IMSA Jaguars in the workshops, let alone test one, made his racing debut at Ingliston aged nineteen, driving a humble MG Midget. Graduating quickly to single-seaters, he soon became Scottish Formula Ford champion, his upwardly mobile progress maintained with some promising outings in Formula 3 in 1970. Then came the chance to join Ecurie Ecosse to race Formula 2 in 1971:

"The only time I got sentimental in my entire motor racing career was when I turned down March to drive for Ecurie Ecosse. It was a disaster. They had no money, no organisation, no nothing."

There were no decent results either, the partnership netting only a ninth place at Brands Hatch in August. At the end of the season they went their separate ways but the damage was done and although Tom would scratch around in the likes of Formula Atlantic and F5000 over the next few years his topline single-seater career was effectively terminated there and then at the hands of Ecurie Ecosse, the strength of competition being such that there was no second chance to shine at that level. If he was to continue in the sport he would need to look elsewhere:

"At the time I was coming up through the ranks motor racing was changing. Before, people were paid to drive racing cars. When all the Brazilians and everybody else started to come in with big sponsorship, all of a sudden it changed over to be how much money you had got to drive the car.

"I never had those sorts of funds; my family never paying for me to go motor racing. I had to generate my money from actually doing it and had been approached by Ford once or twice to drive saloons, but turned it down, preferring to stick with single seaters. But when the Fuel Crisis came along it brought with it the harsh reality of life; I had to earn some money to eat – or starve. So I went and drove for Ford."

After Ford came BMW and the winning the prestigeous Tourist Trophy at Silverstone in 1977, a feat he has since added to three times as a driver, five as a team owner. And it was while contracted to the German marque that Walkinshaw first got directly involved with race car preparation, his expertise then helping Mazda to win the British Saloon Car Championship in both 1980 and 1981, taking the laurels in the mighty Spa 24 Hours in the latter year too.

Running directly alongside the Japanese cars were TWR Rovers. The story of how they came into the Kidlington fold is one that encapsulates the essence of Tom Walkinshaw:

"We were getting paid to run Mazdas in the British series and winning it. One day we sat down and decided that we had to try and run a British car. I had gotten wind of the fact that Rover were about to pull the plug on their programme, such was the lack of success, so I went along and said 'I have looked at your car. If you give me a month I can put two seconds a lap on it.' They were very sceptical so I said 'Okay, I will tell you what I will do. For every tenth of a second I make it go faster, up to a maximum of two seconds, you will give me a certain amount of money.' They agreed.

"I then spent a whole weekend reading all their test reports. They were actually running on, I think it was, 15″ rubber from Michelin, and looking at the reports it was quite obvious 14″ was faster. But when you asked why they continued to use the larger diameter, they said it was because the car 'looked better', it was much more 'aggressive looking'!"

An engineer to the core of his gaelic heart, Tom shakes his head at the memory of it: "Anyway, I came up with a spec, had the induction system sorted out, did everything in two weeks and had it ready for the next race. They were thinking more on two or three months, but I could not wait that long. I delivered it up to them the day before practice at Silverstone – and the car was put on pole position first time out! It went just on three seconds a lap quicker than it had ever done in its life before!"

Of such things are the Walkinshaw legend born.

Then came Jaguar. And as Tom explains the background to his getting involved with the Coventry marque, yet again it reveals a fascinating insight into the modus operandi of one of the shrewdset men in modern motor sport, a true canny Scot:

"I went to John (later Sir John) Egan and told him that, with the regulations for touring cars were changing from Group 1 to Group A, I felt we could develop the car into a winner."

At that time, Jaguar were in turmoil and the throes of emerging from the clutches of the monster that was British Leyland. And now there amidst those hallowed portals was this man with an accent you could cut with a dirk wanting to open up all the old wounds of the ill-fated Broadspeed Coupe programme of the mid-seventies and take Coventry back into racing. With a XJS, to boot. Had he taken too much of the highland juices?

"People laughed at me, I know. All the so-called 'experts'. Only Egan and Neil Johnson (then Sales & Marketing Director) had any belief that we could do it. Eventually we struck a deal in such a way that if we failed Jaguar were distanced enough to be able to deny any involvement whatsoever. It would all be down to a mad Scotsman!

*Davy Jones heads John Nielsen, both drivers having benefited greatly from their association with TWR.*

"But, by the same token, if it was successful then we got paid. They did not have much money at that time, Egan making it very clear that the company was just about bust, so the last thing they had was any money. So I asked for a supply of parts and access into the engineering department for any technical information I needed.

"There was no interference whatsoever. We said 'look it is your motor car, you've tested it, and we want to race a variant of your road car. So you tell us the areas where you experienced problems, and where you think we are going to.' We then drew up a hitlist, people went away and prioritised it and we worked from there. I did not want anyone coming back afterwards saying 'I told you so – if only you had asked – I told you not to do it that way' . . ."

Walkinshaw did it his way and despite starting on the front row and leading its very first ETCC event, results took half a season in coming, but come they did. Winning first at the classic Brno course in the midsummer of 1982, an XJS won

## 'Okay, it was a big lump, but . . .'

four of the last six races that season to claim third in the standings. The next year it was five wins and second place in the big league, the crowning glory coming in 1984 when a magnificent seven victories – including Spa – clinched the Manufacturers' title for Coventry, T.Walkinshaw Esquire coming out top of the Drivers' league. With the Big Cats soon to be neutered by rule changes, it was quite some way to bow out.

Jaguar were Back! But if those self same so-called 'experts' had first considered Tom to be out of order when he first suggested racing a XJS, the thought of making a Group C winner from the venerable old V12 had them shaking their heads in dismay. Touring cars were one thing, sports cars another:

"I had been wanting to go Group C with Jaguar from the outset, but nobody really believed it was possible. We were back into the 'okay, you managed it with the XJS but Group C, well, that is a REAL racing car' syndrome. Nobody believed you could go and win a Group C race with an old production engine. Okay, it was a big lump, but we just had to design a car around it."

Initially there was talk of using the Group 44 cars run with quite some success in IMSA and then seen at Le Mans in 1984/5, but Mr Walkinshaw is adamant that Mr Tullius' beautiful white beasts would never have been suited to Group C and, following more discussions, the go-ahead was finally given to commission the building of

what would become known as the XJR6, forerunner of the 1989 Le Mans XJR9LMs.

"The original car was over-engineered because we could not have a development period in the timescale available so we had to put a little more weight on the car than we wanted. Taking a second hit at it almost at once, we brought out the XJR8 which was much lighter. It was the race car we intended from the beginning. After that, you know the story . . ."

And with that he was gone. Off to the pitlane, then the 'chopper', up, up and away.

They seek him here, they seek him there, they seek Tom Walkinshaw everywhere. . .

*Relaxing with team members just before the start.*

*Wollek and Stuck, the pre-race favourites.*

*Hans Stuck does not need his spectacular helmet design to confirm his stardom, his driving and personality do that.*

*The battle stained Joest Porsche en route to third place.*

# THE TEMPEST

THERE ARE PEOPLE in motor racing who never quite manage a smile, and complain quite a lot about their luck. It's hard to imagine why they are in the sport at all, doubly so when you catch sight of Hans Stuck in the paddock, in the pitlane or doing something extraordinary on the track. . ...

'Hanschen' is the living soul of motor racing, the epitome of the dashing driver. Six feet tall, thinning fair hair standing out as though in shock, with merry grey eyes, usually he is laughing; about a joke he has just played on someone or is about to play. And he is forgiven everything because he is, after all, an outstandingly fine racing driver.

One of my earliest recollections of Hans-Joachim is of viewing the underside of his black Castrol sponsored 'works' BMW CSL at Brünchen, one of the most spectacular parts of the proper Nürburgring. It was 1974. I had gone there with John Dunbar, then of LAT Photographic, on hearing that this crazy German was going higher and higher each time he circulated the 14-mile track and that, sooner or later, his BMW would probably not come down again!

Sure enough, we heard the distinctive sound of the 430-bhp 6-cylinder engine echoing through the trees from Hohe Act and Wipperman, heard the revs lurch as the car left the ground fractions of a moment before it appeared. Yes, the best part of five feet off the ground!

In a way he was famous before he ever sat in a racing car, his father Hans Stuck Senior having been one of Professor Porsche's first contracted Auto-Union drivers. Papa made his name hillclimbing and was never more spectacular than when arm-wrestling his supercharged, mid-engined, twin rear wheeled monster between the banks of Shelsley Walsh or

heading for the clouds at Freiburg. It was at the latter, incidentally, that Stuck Senior handled a so-called Auto-Union P-wagen, a Porsche-wagen, for the last time in 1937, soundly beating Hermann Lang, Rudolf Caracciola and Bernd Rosemayer. And it was at Freiburg again that Hans watched his father, the famous 'Bergmeister', competing in a BMW saloon in 1962.

"He did not want to stop, of course. I was 11 when we went to Freiburg, and I walked to the top of the hill. There, they wrote the times on a tree, and my Daddy was the last to go. Anton Fischaber and Sepp Greger were two well known names to go before him and when Papa made the best time of the day they said 'What do we have to do to beat this old man?' I did not say anything then but when I told Papa he was very pleased! He was 61 years old and could still beat all the youngsters. I'd like to be like that when I'm 61!".

Hans started in saloons in 1969 and got his first break in 1971 with a BMW contract, before defecting to Ford for a couple of years, he and Jochen Mass having started their careers together and run in parallel ever since. Then it was back to BMW through to 1985 when he drove for Porsche for the first time in what he called "a spiritual homecoming".

He went with BMW and March into Formula Two in 1974 and Jochen Neerspach saw to it that he spent three years in the March Grand Prix team as well, although they were powered by Cosworth DFV engines. Disappointing years they were too, with a meagre total of thirteen points, his big chance came in 1977 when Bernie Ecclestone signed him up for the Brabham-Alfa Romeo alongside John Watson.

Two third places, appropriately at the

Nürburgring and again at the Österreichring, and the pleasure of leading briefly at Watkins Glen, made this a good season for Stuck but it ended badly when the then twice world champion Niki Lauda became available for '78 and Hans was 'released' from his contract. There followed two distinctly poor years with Shadow and ATS before he called it a day in single-seaters.

Looking back on it, his Formula One career was a succession of near misses, and he somehow became typecast as a saloon or sports car driver. Motor racing has a rather unkind way of typecasting and since the lanky Bavarian found it almost impossible to fit comfortably into the cockpit unless it was tailored for him, he needed a very secure berth with a top team to show his real talent. It never came about.

Neerspach was his guide and mentor throughout the Seventies, both at Ford and BMW, going on to sign Stuck to lead the new BMW M1 series in 1979. In the next two years the M1 was further developed by March Engineering into a full Group 5 machine and their effort was rewarded when it scored its first, and only, World Championship victory at the Nürburgring in 1981. Having finished third there together twelve months earlier, winners of the wet 1000 kms race were Hans Stuck and Nelson Piquet, winner of the 1980 BMW M1 Procar Championship. Nor was there any secret that Neerspach hoped to steer BMW into designing a three-litre V8 which would fit neatly into the central engine bay (or into an F.1. car) but that is quite another story. . ...

When Neerspach left BMW at the end of 1979 the light seemed to go out for Hans Stuck as well. The M1 programme kept him going but it was Piquet who was the beneficiary of the company's four-cylinder turbo power in his Brabham for 1982, going on to win the World championship with it a year later. Almost on principle Ecclestone would not have an 'old' driver back in the team and Stuck had to ride out a touring car contract with a waiver to drive for his old friend Walter Brun in World Championship sports car racing. In 1982 there was a Sauber Cosworth C6, fast but extremely fragile, followed by Stuck's "black year" of 1983 when the new Brun Motorsport Sehcar-Porsche made its debut at Le Mans.

"Oh, I will never forget *THAT*" he groans. "First Harald Grohs went out and lost a door, then 'Walti' lost the engine cover. Then I went out and had the rear suspension break. All in one evening!". I can remember it too, for Hans had been through a terrible few moments and he stormed back in to the pits in a rare temper. "*YOU* can drive it, I'm finished!" he raged to me, a unique occasion when I was offered a Le Mans drive but was unable to accept. That is how it felt at the time, anyway. . .

Brun saw the light, as it were, in 1984 and brought a customer Porsche 956, at last allowing Stuck to show his true form, winning at Imola, and that long-awaited Porsche 'works' drive duly followed in 1985. The season did not start well as Porsche were struggling a bit with micro-chip settings, the fuel allocation having been reduced 15% from the previous season, but partnered with Derek Bell they finished third at Le Mans and then found the winning groove with victories at Hockenheim, Mosport Park and Brands Hatch.

Their season ended with a shared World Championship for Drivers', the Bavarian amusing everyone when he returned to the Kent circuit a year later with a tee-shirt sporting the legend: "I'm Stuck with Bell". The partnership

was of a rare quality, Hans with electrifying speed in qualifying, Derek with pace to match on race consumption coupled with complete reliability. 1986 was not quite so good for the German, missing out on a second title on a count-back system, but there was handsome compensation when he, Bell and Al Holbert won the Le Mans 24 Hours in their Rothmans Porsche 962C, a high achievement they repeated in 1987. Last year, with Klaus Ludwig replacing the American, Stuck and Bell just missed out on a memorable hat-trick when coming second to the winning Jaguar by less than three minutes.

"I like to race here very much" he said a few days before this year's event. "It is one of the three big happenings in the year: Le Mans, Indianapolis, Monte Carlo. As a racing driver you should win one of these to be very successful, and now I am looking for my third victory.

"Before I drove for Porsche I always wondered why these cars are so difficult to beat. I thought they were nothing special – but now I know the answer! The cars are so well developed, so

reliable, that is exactly what you need here.

"The car is so nice, so easy to drive – down the straight it feels like a Mercedes 500, it really does. You see the Jaguars bouncing around, they must be very hard to drive. They are very fast on the straight but not so good in the corners and their big advantage is to have four cars. They have four chances, we have just one, because I do not think there is another Porsche as good as ours".

As to the circuit itself, he is positive that the place must not be changed fundamentally, and in particular the straight must be left alone. "That is something special to Le Mans, something you don't have at other tracks. If you want to slow the cars down you must have three or four chicanes and that is three or four more chances to have accidents".

Born on New year's Day in 1951, 'Hanschen' will celebrate his fortieth birthday when FISA's new championship begins officially. His chances of getting back into Formula One are virtually extinct, as he well knows, but he will have a full five more years at the top in sports car racing, perhaps ten . . . or twenty, if he follows his father's example.

"My Daddy was beating all the youngsters when he was in his sixties. He enjoyed the sport and had lots of motivation. Well, I have too. I enjoy racing more than ever because I understand it so much better now. In the past five or six years I have driven for such professional teams that they make me feel very good, they make me happy . . . I don't want anything else. Racing has always been central to my life, there was never anything else. Well, when I was young I did think only about going into the mountains and yodelling. But I grew out of that. . ."

# MEASURE FOR MEASURE

## Jaguar

THE FOUR Silk Cut cars present at Le Mans '89 showed to be the following chassies: Car#1 –588, Car#2 –688, Car#3 –288 and Car#4 –287. Historically the most interesting was the third car, built as it was around the 1988 Daytona 24 Hours winning monocoque and especially flown in for the occasion. It could be readily distinguished from the others by virtue of (blanked off) air-jack holes just behind each front wheel.

Early in the week, Jaguar designer Tony Southgate summed up the technical aspects of this year's Le Mans effort by explaining: "All four cars are very much the same as the winning car from last year. There is a different tail section – the air intake on the roof has disappeared – and slight differences in the nose. The rest is just in chassis settings which are very similar to the winning car from last year. A bit less drag, a bit more horsepower; in theory it should be a bit quicker. That's basically it."

Throughout practice all the cars carried wire mesh over their NACA side intakes but this was discarded for race day, one learned team member commenting that this simple expediency was worth "a couple of hundred revs" down Mulsanne.

## The Porsches

"IT IS EIGHTY per cent a 'works' car" said Hans Stuck about his Joest #9, continuing: "It is a brand new chassis (962 145) built at the factory and having all the latest equipment with carbon fibre anti-roll bars and the latest springs. The only main difference between last year's factory cars and this one is that it is now on Goodyear tyres which have a tremendous lot of grip in the rear, are nice down the straights and at least as good as Dunlop were last year".

There was no sign of the revised front oil cooler/centre post rear wing aerodynamics seen so successfully in the Super-Cup and also at Dijon, while Joest were also represented by –004, an ex-works car now the regular mount of Jean-Louis Ricci and friends, plus –007, this being the 'Wollek' car from last year's Le Mans 'works' effort. And as if to reiterate their allegiance to Weissach, all three ran on Speedline wheels, just as the factory cars always used to.

Of the other two 1988 'works' chas-

sies, Vern Schuppan had the ex-Andretti family –008 in Omron colours while –010 (which came second) was left behind in Kremer's Cologne workshops – still in its Shell/Dunlop livery – as the brothers elected to bring two of their new Thompson built aluminium CK6 tubs instead, reckoning the metal variety to be better suited to the rigours of the 24 Hours than any 'plastic' version.

Schuppans's other entry was another from Stuttgart's latest production run (as opposed to his own recently laid down batch) while Repsol Brun #17, plated 962 150, is deemed to be the latest Typ 962 to date.

All the remaining seventeen Porsches present were generally very much as previously seen, with Brun's FromA #5 and Alpha #6 both of honeycomb construction with composite panels, again courtesy of John Thompson, who was also responsible for the ex-Kremer machine now operated by Almeras. Number #5 was unique in using 'Bombien' sidepanels, everyone else featuring a variety of differing styles, the older cars generally having an earlier type of tail section than seen on later cars.

Richard Lloyd brought two of his unique Nigel Stroud designed devices, the black PCGB/Raika example only being turned from a bare tub into a Le Mans runner in the seven days before the event. Noticably different from more conventional 962s, modellers will keenly note that although both ran with special curved radiator air intakes early

in the week, they raced with more familiar straight edged versions.

## The Japanese

NIGEL STROUD was also responsible for the latest offerings of Mazda, sole runners in the IMSA GTP category. Now in revised 767B format, they featured one of this year's most interesting technical aspects with their newly developed variable induction system as fitted to the four-rotor engines. An onboard computer varies the equivelent length of the air inlet pipes subject to engine speed and load, thereby helping torque especially in the low/mid range. Allied to increased use of ceramics and special alloys, Mazda claimed a 15% improvement in engine efficiency. It would serve them well.

Toyota had also been hard at work on engines, the new 3.2 litre turboed V8 claimed to output 950 bhp in Qualifying trim, 1060 during bench testing! Three 89CVs would arrive with the new units, two 88Cs featuring the old straight four.

"One thing you have to remember" said lead driver Geoff Lees: "is that our new car is not built by March or Lola or anybody else, but Toyota. It is our own car, we have built everything. It is the first time we have done so and straightaway the car is competitive."

Nissan, on the other hand, owed their allegiance to Lola, manufacturers of the

*Powering a winner, five litres of turbocharged Mercedes Benz V8.*

*The supposedly fragile Hewland gearbox stood the race well, post-Qualifying modifications proving to be decisive.*

all new composite R89C, the outdated old Marches now a thing of the past although one privateer version was present to haunt them and being run under the Courage banner. Using three litres of Electramotive V6 whereas the new cars relied on 3.2 litres of the latest twin turboed Weslake-attended V8, its most notable technical advance since being discarded by the 'works' was probably to have no less than four rear-view mirrors!

Showing their commitment to the future rather than what was now behind them, the new Howard Marsden Keith Greene led venture also had Don Devendorf and Trevor Harris of the omnipotent IMSA champions on hand to help their cause. That the new cars were not yet equipped with carbon fibre brakes would be highlighted early in the race . . .

## Sauber Mercedes

AS WITH EVERYONE else, the aerodynamics on all their four cars were refined since last year and showed subtle changes from the normal sprint car trim, with a lower rear wing etc, but the most visible change was the addition of a snorkel to help direct cooling air onto the drivers.

Car #61 would race –04, Car#62 use –02 while Car#63 had –03. In practice, –05 had also been run, in lieu of –02, to set the pole position time, its spec-sheet including special carbon fibre brakes not found on the racers. Car #63 would also start (but not finish) the race with a yellow outer left-sided headlamp, the others all being clear.

## Aston Martin

RETURNING TO La Sarthe as a fully fledged 'works' effort for the first time since their victory thirty years ago, driver Brian Redman summed up matters thus: "It has some very good features; the brakes are superb, the engine extremely nice, the gearbox works well. It is very comfortable on the Mulsanne without any movement at all, going through the Kink without any twitch or tremor, without any thought of having to lift off the throttle.

"From the beginning we saw signs of it not having enough speed, something which was confirmed at Dijon three weeks ago. We have some aerodynamic and weight problems to solve, being 40 kph slower than either Jaguar and Mercedes. Top speed is not the be-all and end-all, it is the acceleration from the previous corner which counts, so every time we come out of a corner we are dropping behind aerodynamically. There is a lot of work to do. We will be very happy to finish, but quite lucky to do so."

Noted as Car#18/chassis –02 and Car#19/chassis –03, both have a very high angle of incidence for their American tuned engines.

## The French

WM SECATEVA were upholding French honour for the last time with a brace of their now familiar Peugeot engined projectiles. Meanwhile, besides the old March Nissan, Yves Courage also entered two of his latest Porsche powered C1 specials, designated C22LMs, with a detuned C20LM in the C2 class, this apparently being the car which came third overall only two years ago. None featured anything particularly new or remarkable over previous appearances, only ALD offering anything by way of innovation au Francais with their composite Cosworth powered C289, this being a veritable rose amongst the wilted thorns of three outmoded BMW engined devices allied to aluminium hardware the marque also sported.

## Spice

TWO C1 Spices were present, new exhausts and starter motor more to rectify earlier problems than anything specific for Le Mans. Amongst the seven Spice C2s, only the second Chamberlain entry with its familiar Hart turbo was other than Cosworth V8 powered. Lombardi chose to race without its nosesplitter while Mako had last year's refettled championship winner.

## The Others

ITALY, once the driving force of the Le Mans race, were represented by only a solus entry of a much outdated design from Lancia, albeit built around a new Dallara chassis.

Down in C2, the 1989 aluminium/carbon fibre Tigas were notably sleeker than earlier examples, front mounted radiators helping the effect. The singleton Argo and ADA entries were much as before, the West London device – constructed by March Engineering – sporting a drilled rear crossmember and, for the race, box sections over the sidepanel mounted radiator inlets.

# CAR DATA FILE

| MAKE | MODEL | LENGTH | WIDTH | HEIGHT | W/BASE | F/TRACK | R/TRACK | ENGINE TYPE | CAPACITY (cc) | BHP |
|------|-------|--------|-------|--------|--------|---------|---------|-------------|---------------|-----|
| ADA | 02 | 4735 | 1990 | 960 | N/A | 1530 | 1470 | Cosworth V8 | 3300 | 500 |
| ALD | BMW | 4300 | 1920 | 1050 | 2550 | 1500 | 1460 | BMW S6 | 3500 | 455 |
| ALD | C289 | N/A | N/A | 1050 | 2670 | 1530 | 1490 | Cosworth V8 | 3300 | 530 |
| Argo | JM19C | 4500 | 1900 | 1000 | 2700 | 1480 | 1480 | Cosworth V8 | 3300 | 500 |
| Aston M | AMR-1 | 4775 | 1987 | 1016 | 2896 | 1600 | 1524 | Aston M. V8 | 6000 | 650 |
| Cougar | C20LM | 4800 | 1990 | 1050 | 2600 | 1500 | 1520 | Porsche F6t | 2800 | 650 |
| Cougar | C22LM | 4800 | 1990 | 1050 | 2710 | N/A | N/A | Porsche F6t | 3000 | 750 |
| Jaguar | XJR9LM | 4800 | 2000 | 1100 | 2780 | 1500 | 1450 | Jaguar V12 | 7000 | 730 |
| Lancia | LC2 | 4795 | 1995 | 1040 | 2665 | 1616 | 1564 | Ferrari V8 | 3050 | 800 |
| Mazda | 767B | 4683 | 1990 | 1013 | 2637 | 1584 | 1504 | Mazda 4r | 650 | 630 |
| Nissan | R89C | 4800 | 1990 | 1100 | 2794 | N/A | N/A | Nissan V8t | 3500 | 800 |
| Porsche | 962C | 4770 | 1990 | 1080 | 2795 | 1634 | 1590 | Porsche F6t | 3000 | 770 |
| Porsche | 962GTi | 4800 | 2000 | 1030 | 2795 | 1648 | 1548 | Porsche F6t | 3000 | 640 |
| Sauber | C9/88 | 4800 | 1980 | 1070 | 2700 | 1616 | 1550 | Mercedes V8t | 5000 | 720 |
| Spice C2 | SE88C | 4550 | 1820 | 1020 | 2660 | 1480 | 1460 | Cosworth V8 | 3300 | 550 |
| Spice C1 | SE89C | 4775 | 1898 | 1028 | 2717 | 1490 | 1475 | Cosworth V8 | 3300 | 600 |
| Tiga | GC289 | 4670 | 1880 | 1070 | 2590 | 1520 | 1420 | Cosworth V8 | 3300 | 500 |
| Toyota | 88CV | 4625 | 1990 | 1040 | 2700 | 1600 | 1575 | Toyota S4t | 2140 | 680 |
| Toyota | 89CV | 4790 | 1940 | 1015 | 2725 | 1560 | 1540 | Toyota V8t | 3200 | 800 |
| WM | P88 | 4490 | 1995 | 1020 | 2500 | 1520 | 1420 | Peugeot V6t | 2850 | 850 |

NB: All measurements are in millimetres, as extracted from official press packs etc. Engines are atmospheric except where designated t/turbocharged, r/rotary. Note how different manufacturers/teams interpret power outputs!

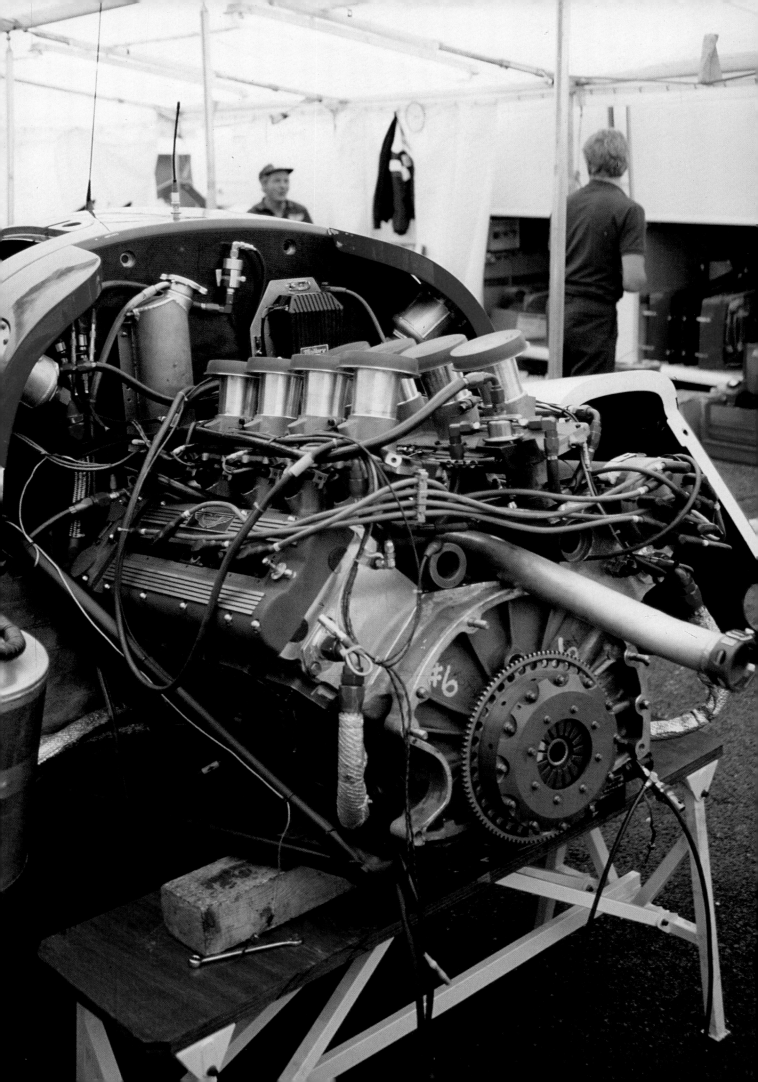

# THROUGH THE LOOKING GLASS

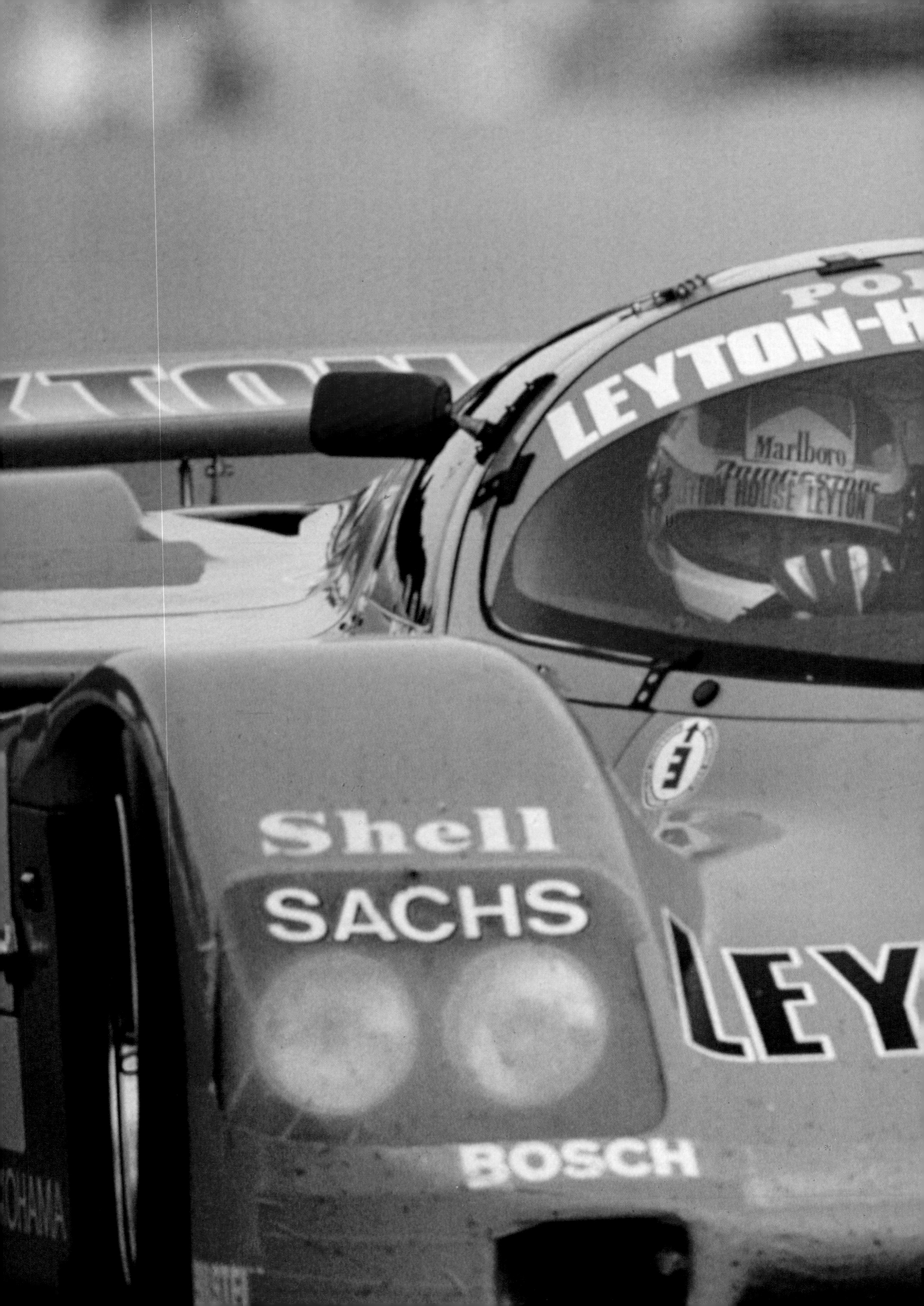
LEYTON-H
LEYTON
Marlboro
Shell
SACHS
LEY
BOSCH

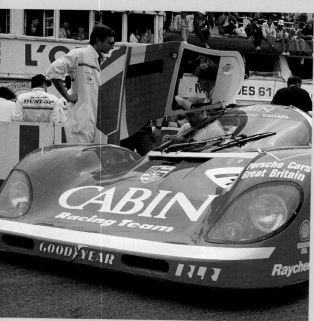

44

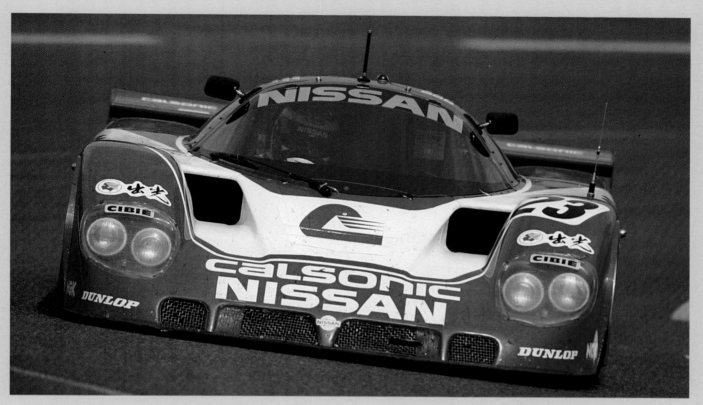

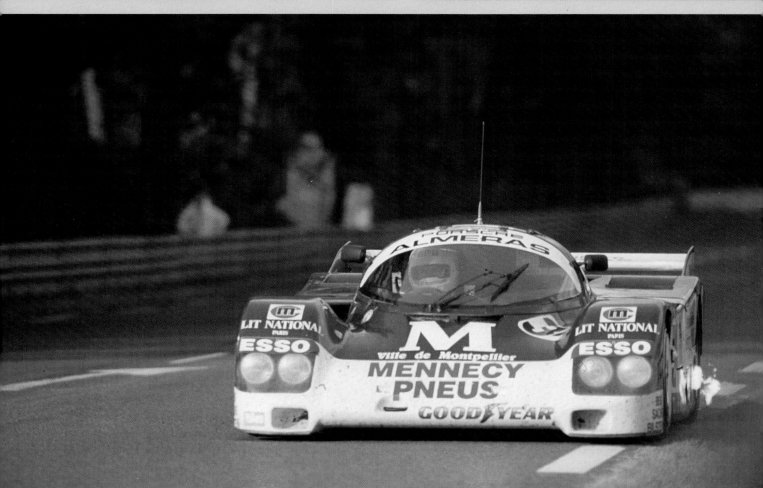

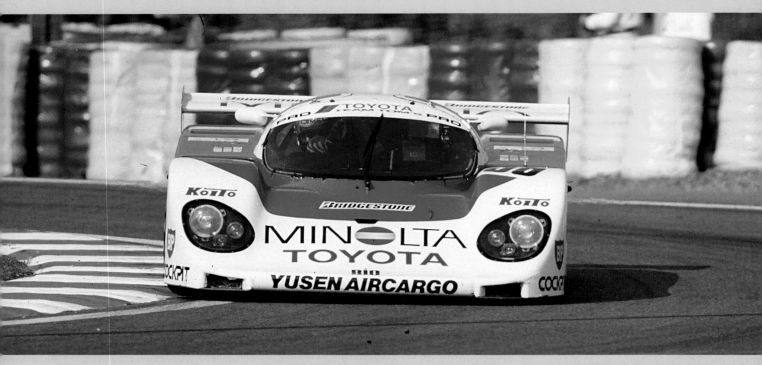

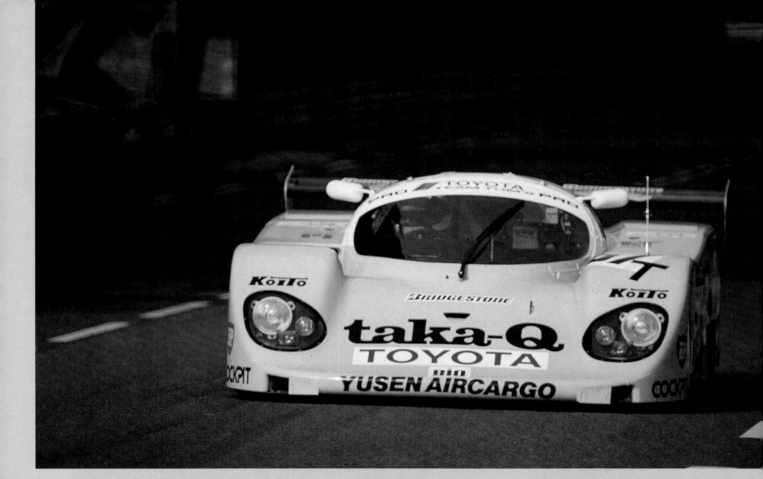

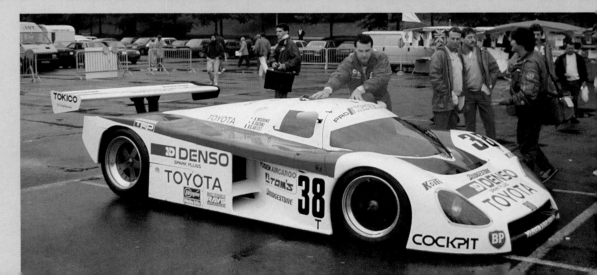

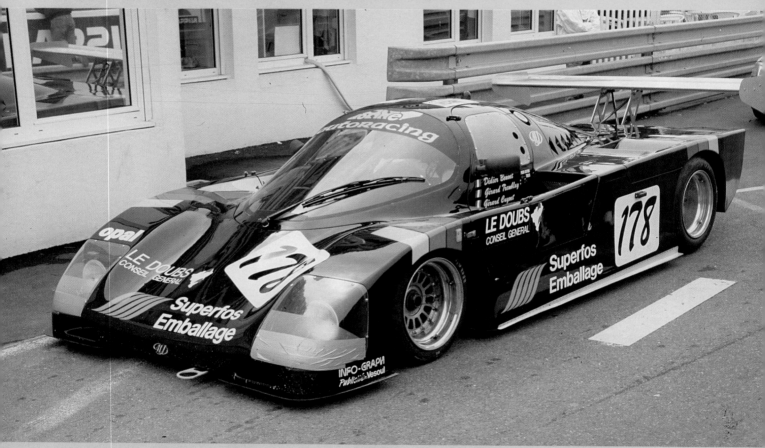

# A MIDSUMMER NIGHT'S DREAM    (Part 1)

*To sleep perchance to dream.*
*To dream the dreams of the innocent.*

CURLED UP in the passenger seat of his father's car, the youngest member of the Heybridge Heroes had slept the journey away. Only ten years old yet soon to be a veteran of his third Le Mans 24 Hours, he, like every other member of the Purple Army descending on the French city that week, was keen for Jaguar to repeat the win of twelve months back. Would his dream come true, or would it be a nightmare? Only time would tell.

They had come by boat, arrived by 'plane, in cars of every size. So had those favouring Porsche and Mercedes et al. As it was, there were nigh on a quarter of a million people present by the time Oscar Larrauri posted the best time of Saturday morning's Warm-Up session, all four XJRs in the next six, the interlopers being the 'British' Nissan and Schlesser, the pink 962 noticable only by its absence. If Porsche were sandbagging then this was of Sahara proportions . . .

A weak sun in a bland sky suggested it would be cool, a shower of overnight rain having taken the heat out of the morning, only the sight of Hawaiian Tropic girls and Mazda maidens bringing any appreciable rise in temperature as race time fast approached. Pouting and preening, parades and oompah, there was all the normal fun of the fair.

'Schless' was busy giving umpteen interviews at one end of the grid, Robin Donovan waiting quietly and patiently at the other. Tom Walkinshaw just sat on the guardrail with members of his team, having seen it all before. Amongst the newcomers, Don Shead smiled as he savoured the atmosphere for the first time, Lyn St.James looking wide-eyed and innocent at the magnitude of it all. It was, without doubt, a long way from her piano playing days in the St.Louis conservatoire of music.

And soon the sound was of engines. One, then another, then another, gradually the slumbering giants were awakening, the deep throated roar emanating from each just a fraction of their strength. Only the FromA 962 failed to join in, it's flat-six not coming to terms with the task ahead until all the rest had set out on the pace lap, Harold Grohs required to do a lot of catching up even before the event had actually started.

*They'e Off! Mauro Baldi already had the advantage as the field hurtles towards the Dunlop Curve.*

HUGH CHAMBERLAIN (Spice #101/102): "The #101 car went 2½ seconds quicker in the Warm-Up than during Qualifying. On full tanks with its race settings. At the moment I think we are about eleven seconds per lap quicker than the next best in race trim so you try stopping a Spaniard going quickly. It's impossible!"

DON SHEAD (Spice #171): "It is incredible, everything it is cracked up to be. The circuit is unbelievable, the parades all part of the show. It's what makes Le Mans what it is!".

ROSS CHEEVER (Toyota #36): "I do not know about the pits here but the women are nice! I've only done five laps so am going to have to learn it during the race. It's pretty exciting. It's work, I guess!".

As the Mercedes pace car pulled off to the right, its racing cousins accelerated as one, a huge cloud of dust and smoke billowing in their wake, a roar of approval emanating from the cheering crowd. Headlong past the pits and into the first corner, Baldi swept across from the left to lead Schlesser, Jan Lammers tucking in behind Jean-Louis, the three other Jaguars in line astern on the outside. Wollek followed the Dutchman while Larrauri was monstering his Repsol 962 straight through the middle, aiming for a gap which was forever closing around him. Further back Jelinski had gotten a flier in his Porsche, the group he led also including both Kremers, a pair of fast starting Nissans and the third Sauber.

Through the chicane and under the Dunlop Bridge, Mercedes led Mercedes, Davy Jones squeezing the 'American' Jag-wah into third, Lammers then Larrauri next in line. And when all were safely passed out came the WM Peugeot,

last but not least on this three thousand mile journey into the unknown.

One long ribbon of hue and cry, they threaded their way through the Esses, safely around Tertre Rouge and headed out for the first time in anger down Mulsanne, forty thousand screaming horses let off the leash and raring to go. A multi-coloured blur of speed, down that most famous strip of black tarmacadam they went, jinking and jostling in their efforts to gain an early advantage, the afternoon sun dancing merrily through the trees and throwing long shadows across their path.

Up front, Mauro kept a small gap over his team mate, the pair of silver streamliners hugging the right hand side of the track as they went. Blindingly fast, taking the bumps and dips in their stride, approaching the flat-in-fifth Kink Jaguar #3 suddenly flicked out left from third position and past Schlesser into second spot. Duane Davy Jones was on a charge.

While British hopes took an early set-back, everyone else went around again, Baldi leading Jones, leading Schlesser, leading Nielsen, the Nissan getting ever closer as Bailey piled on the pressure. Then came Ferte, Larrauri, Wollek and Mass, every one of them keen not to be left behind as the pace grew hotter.

By the time the front runners got onto Mulsanne for the second time Jones was riding with Number 61, the Silk Cat hard on the silver heels of its quarry. Down the straight they went as if attached by a short invisible rope, two hundred, two-ten, two-twenty, more, Italian mirrors full of New York's finest. And just as he did to 'Schless' last time, so Davy did to Mauro this, pulling alongside as they lined up for the Kink . . .

Ditto John Nielsen and Julian Bailey; Jaguar #2 ahead of team leader Lammers by the time they rounded Mulsanne Corner, the Nissan also going through on the sweep down to Indianapolis. Suspecting a punctured tyre, Jan would stop at the end of the opening lap for fresh rubber, his Le Mans'89 not getting off to anywhere near the euphoria which ended Le Mans'88.

And coming in behind him was Aston Martin #19, David Leslie dismounting while a dashboard fire was investigated. Not the most auspicious of starts one could have wished for the Newport Pagnell Flyer, he would take the V8 thunder box back out again while things were fixed, returning soon to have the electronic readouts refitted before finally getting underway in earnest.

*Andy Wallace heads towards the Dunlop Bridge early on. There would be no repeat victory for him or Jaguar #2.*

. . . and into the lead. Last year it had taken half a dozen laps for a Jaguar to lead Le Mans, on this occasion but two.

Around the rest of the lap Jones held on to his advantage, the huge television screen at Virage Ford giving the awaiting crowd an electronic view of proceedings, the purple predator's dash through that same complex soon afterwards confirming the state of play for their own eyes. Roaring past the grandstands and enclosures on Pits Straight, fifty thousand British voices rose as one to herald the achievement, their joy amplified when finding 'Super John' having moved up into third.

Yet although out on the terraces the mood was optimistic, the expectations sky high, in the pits TWR team personnel were less convinced. For sure they now had first and third but soon they would also have the last two as well, Ferte peeling off to investigate a similar problem to that which had delayed Lammers half a lap. Nothing untoward was found so he was soon on his way again, but the question mark remained.

Jag, Merc, Jag, Merc; Bailey was still fifth and closing, Larrauri now sixth, Wollek, Mass, Jelinski and Geoff Brabham filling out the top ten. The Schuppan and Kremer's mixed and matched behind them, Lees in there too for Toyota.

Third time down Mulsanne it was Nielsen's turn for a shot at Baldi, outbreaking him into the corner to make it a Jaguar one-two. Oh, how The Purple Army were going to love this!

*The pole position car was in trouble almost from the start. Here 'Schless' makes a point during an early stoppage.*

Even more daring, Julian Bailey dived inside Schlesser at the Kink to demote the pole-car down to fifth, taking Baldi when they surged side by side into the Dunlop Curve as everyone went out to start their fourth tour of the French countryside. And it did not take much longer for Wollek to push the pink Porsche ahead of the Saubers too, all three of which were now running nose to tail, their qualifying glories a thing of the past.

Quickly closing the gap to the battle for second place, Bob had a fine view of the Nissan hounding the Jaguar as they sped along Mulsanne in high speed convoy. Already the guys on Radio Le Mans were trying to figure out how long it would be before the Japanese car led Le Mans.

But the 'Curse of the Commentators' got to it first. As Nielsen reached the bottom of the straight and turned into the right hander by the signalling posts, Bailey was closer still, too close. Locking up as he did so, having 'gotten on the binders' Julian had careered into the back of Jaguar #2, the suspect steel brakes on the Nissan having let him down badly. Although he would eventually manhandle the crippled machine back to the pits its short and spectacular race was run, a suspension arm having been pushed back into the chassis. Sayonara, Bailey-san.

The savage attack on the Jaguar's rear had left it more than a little mauled, the following pack all taking advantage of its plight as Nielsen cruised in to have the damage inspected, his Le Mans luck having again run out early, Tom Walkinshaw again left to mutter lurid Highland oaths about how for the second consecutive 24 Hours race his team's chances had been thwarted by early contact with a Nissan. No wee timorous beastie he, TW would make quite plain to the man with the microphone in his hand as to who he thought responsible for the metal bender – and it wasn't the Dane.

All this kerfuffel promoted the Joest Porsche into second with the three Saubers now in line astern filling the positions down to fifth. Never in need of inspiration when behind the wheel, nonetheless it seemed as if a spur to Wollek's efforts and soon he could be seen riding the kerbs and sliding the tail out in his pursuit of happiness that is leader shaped, headlamps blazing in the afternoon sun. It was spectacular stuff. Not that Jones was likely to surrender the advantage to him easily, the American already having taken on the mantle Lammers aspired to so successfully last year and, even so early into the event, seeming determined to win the race from the front.

Fermin Velez was hoping for similar things from his own Silk Cut liveried device too, the Chamberlain Spice #101 having led the class from the first lap and already half a mile clear of its C2 pursuers who were led by Lombardi, twenty-third and thirty-second overall respectively, Yorino heading the Mazda class in #202. Others were not so fortunate, ADA losing the first of two doors which would disappear in short order, a misfire spoiling the early run of the Leyton House 962, the WM Peugeot was making the first so many unscheduled stoppages you would be forgiven for thinking it was on wildcat strike.

Mauro Baldi was the first front-runner to make a planned pit call, coming in as he did after thirty-one minutes, Kenny Acheson sent on his way with the minimum of fuss. Unfortunately for Brun, Larrauri could not emulate the slickness of the feat, overshooting his pits and having to back up sharply before work could commence. Then came Mass and Jelinski with the rest of the leaders in swift order, Wollek last to do so after enjoying one lap of glory out front before handing over to Hans Stuck with forty-four minutes on the clock.

Tyres on, fuel in, up and away; when the first round of routine stops were over and done with and everything had settled down once again, Jaguar #3 still led, now by about half a minute from Jochen Mass who was doing a great job keeping Sauber #63 in second place ahead of Stuck, the Porsche once sneaking in front as they turned on to the Mulsanne, Jochen retaking the position by the time they got to the other end. Jelinski was fourth followed by Larrauri, the other two Mercedes' next in line. Then came the surviving Nissans, split by Lammers, the Dutchman rapidly making up for time lost with that early delay, his pitstop routine now out of synch-, Ferte fourteenth, Nielsen way back in twentieth having lost a full lap having his XJR's wounds healed following that earlier contretemps. And the Chamberlain Spice #101 still led C2.

By the time everyone came back for seconds nearly an hour and a half had gone and still the Jaguar maintained its advantage, was even extending it, while Mass was needing to use all his guile to fend off the continuing advances of Stuck, despite the fact that the Saubers seemed intent on maintaining a fixed race pace rather than be drawn into any heroics. With a question mark still hanging over the longevity of their gearboxes it seemed a wise policy.

*Dominic Dobson brings the Takefuji 962 in after being put into the barriers by Wollek. It was a portent of things to come. . .*

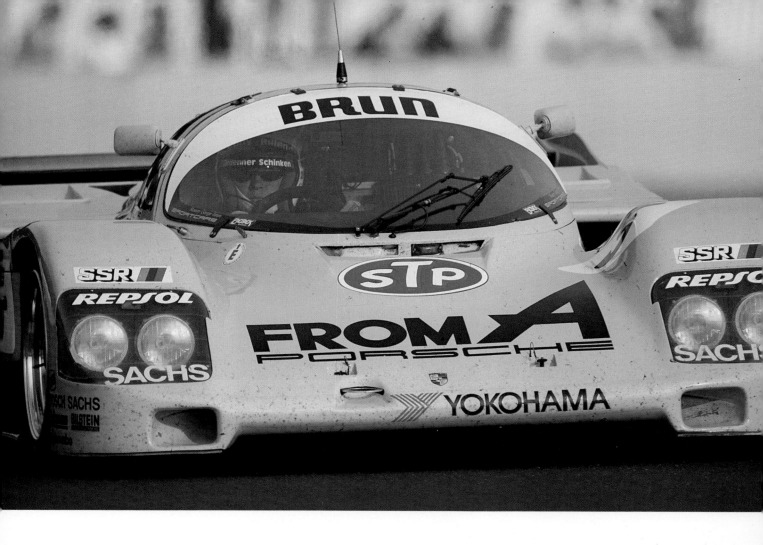

*The From-A 962 of Grohs/Nakaya/van der Merwe started ninth but would be out of the race come sunset with electrical problems.*

Then disaster struck for Sauber Mercedes #63. Shortly after taking over from the former Grand Prix ace, Manual Reuter hit a stray exhaust pipe while at full tilt down the big straight, two unscheduled stops being required to check the holed underbody and collect a new nosecone. This put what had seemed to be the best of the Swiss machines out of immediate contention back in twentieth, just behind the Nielsen/Wallace/Cobb car. Carrying on regardless, it is possible to come back from there, mused the pundits, Ludwig and Pescarolo had proved that in '84, but not many fancied their chances the way this race was panning out. You would have to look elsewhere for your winner this time, of that there was no doubt . . .

But not as far as Toyota #38, the Nippodenso machine looking somewhat battered and bewildered after Hoshino bounced it off the armco, the red and white livery matching his embarrassment, especially when Didier Artzet declared it undrivable after only one more cautious exploratory lap. With a Nissan out and now a Toyota, the sun was already starting to set on the challenge from the Land of the Rising Sun.

Nor was Hoshino the only Oriental casualty of the early going, Iketani blotting his copybook again when losing control almost immediately he took over

the Davey Porsche, his tenure in the team short but decidedly not sweet. 'Kats' had used up all of his nine lives and would not be seen again, repairs taking over an hour. Meanwhile, elsewhere, ADA were suffering as well, those two lost doors only a prelude to failed electrics, while the Leyton House 962 was still in trouble, its problems soon due to be terminal when Sekiya crashed in the Porsche Curves to the severe detriment of Kremer's newest chassis. It would be repairable, but not here, not today.

While the toll was starting to be taken, Spice #108 and various Brunmobiles amongst those seeing a lot of the pitlane in those opening hours, Derek Daly had taken over the leading car, Silk Cut #3, and continued to pull away, the Porsches of Stuck and Raphanel (in for Jelinski) leading the pursuit. Behind the Joest pair, Tambay and Salazar were mixing it with the Nissans and the two healthiest Saubers in the next group. And the Chamberlain Spice #101 still led C2.

As the three hour mark approached so did some dark clouds, the long warm afternoon now noticably cooler as the crowds started to disperse to seek their nightly pleasures and sustenances in whatever way turned them on. It would be a long night's journey into day and not only for those on the race track.

But before the hour was struck, Derek Bell was, metaphorically, with the sight of one of his Lloyd Porsche's wheels bounding down Mulsanne before him! Half a dozen laps into his stint, shadowing the top dozen at a full 200 mph plus, 'Dinger' had just negotiated Tertre Rouge when it happened, the problem later traced to being a faulty airgun. Not that the MBE knew the reason why at that time, nevertheless he decided against parking his three wheeled wagon at Les Hunaudieres to order an early supper, chosing instead to make it back to the pits for a replacement and an explanation. Once there, underwhelmed by the experience of it all, Derek's comments filled Radio Le Mans' airwaves with a colourful overflow of vitriol, Richard Lloyd last seen heading for 100.6FM in pursuit of a transcript . . .

Someone else not full of the joys of summer at that moment was one Derek Daly. Over fifty seconds clear of the pack, he too had turned through Tertre Rouge and found his whole world going nowhere in particular, the gearbox jammed in neutral. Gliding to a halt, the Irishman pulled himself out from the steamy cockpit and began to work on the offending object, the plot thickening when he managed to engage reverse rather than any forward gear. As precious racing-losing time trickled away, eventually Derek found second, coaxed the lifeless V12 into action and set about crawling back to the pits for more longterm repairs, his twenty-five minutes stranded out in the country soon to be doubled as the TWR crew went about their business. With two cars having suffered those early tyre dramas, another the innocent victim of a mugging, and now this, if Silk Cut Jaguar were to win this one they were going to have to do it the hard way.

---

DEREK DALY (Jaguar #3): "The linkage broke inside the gearbox, just as I came out of third gear. Being stopped in neutral I had no drive, so I had to get out and fix it with a pair of vice-grips. What took so long was that I did not know what gears were what and got reverse. I did not fancy going backwards – even though I'm an Irishman! – so I had to do the whole thing again, eventually getting second gear.

"It put us too far behind to ever catch up again but the car was very good. I could pull out a lead and still drive to the fuel, only being one per cent over half way through my stint, which was really good. That's the way it goes."

As were Mercedes. While Sauber #63 was racing to make up lost time, Cudini had also been in trouble, making contact with Ross Hyett's Mako Spice to the detriment of its rear wing, #61 having also been in the wars, first clouting a C2 then a Brun Porsche, the damage slight but enough to upset the handling thereafter, Baldi, Acheson and 'Branca' hanging on gamely in fourth place.

The people to benefit most from all these goings on were Joest Porsche once again, Stuck and Wollek taking over top slot at Daly's demise, two minutes clear of Jag #1, with the Jelinski car now third in line but losing ground to Silk Cut #4 in which Alain Ferte was fast making a name for himself. Not that Jaguar's difficulties were behind them, Lammers soon to lose more time with a broken exhaust to make it an early one-two for the Reinhold expresses, his 'oldies but goldies' 962 for Pescarolo and friends running in gently-gently mode in around twelfth spot, marking time for a late charge should they still be handily placed come breakfast. Joest, Joest and more Joest; it was all starting to look good for the pre-race favourites.

And even worse for the Japanese. Soon after Sekiya had his Leyton House come tumbling down around him, the Minolta Toyota lost its engine, the last vestiges of hope for Team Toms finally disappearing when the Earl of Dumfries threw the Taka-Q attired version into the Porsche Curves only for it to come out looking very second hand, high speed contact with unyielding armco decidedly not haute couture in the summer of '89.

Trying to hobble in, Johnny got only as far as the Ford Chicane before a driveshaft gave way, his lordship then spending the next hour trying to repair both his honour and the stricken turbocar, the whole sorry episode culminating

in farce when a television cameraman who persisted in getting in everybody's way had his expensive equipment mortally wounded after it became tangled in the Toyota's rear end as JD tried in vain to move off, the twenty metres he managed no good for the Toyota, markedly less so for a bouncing camcorder. No doubt the cameraman had learned one lesson, Dumfries another, Toyota the grim realisation that they would have to wait another year before coming to terms with The Great Race.

Not far away, in the relative calm of the paddock, the huge two-storey press centre erected in optimistic anticipation of the marque's efforts was soon silent and empty, a hand-written message attached to its doors simply announcing that it was 'Closed'. That said it all.

It was fast becoming a race of incident, Dumfries' party piece being shown on the big screen adjacent to his plight only until being rudely interrupted by the horrific sight of a Porsche on fire. Dominic Dobson, one of those 'coming men' who will surely dominate the next era of American racing, had taken over the Takefuji 962 only to have the whole rear end erupt in flames as he accelerated out of Mulsanne Corner. Travelling at some 150 mph when the conflagration engulfed the cherry red coachwork, burning away the brakepipes, Dobson had to run it against the barriers to slow the wayward beast down, coming to an eventual stop not a moment too soon. Word had it that a fuel line may have been fractured following earlier contact with Wollek . . .

. . . who by now had eased clear of he pack, the quarter distance resume revealing them to be a lap and a half up on Joest's Blaupunkt #7 with the Irish/Italian Sauber half the length of Mulsanne further back. As for Jaguar, Lammers et al were fourth and the Ferte/

Headlamps blazing in the afternoon sun, Davy Jones was the star of the early going, taking the lead after two laps.

An early pitstop for veterans Pescarolo/ Ricci/Ballot-Lena.

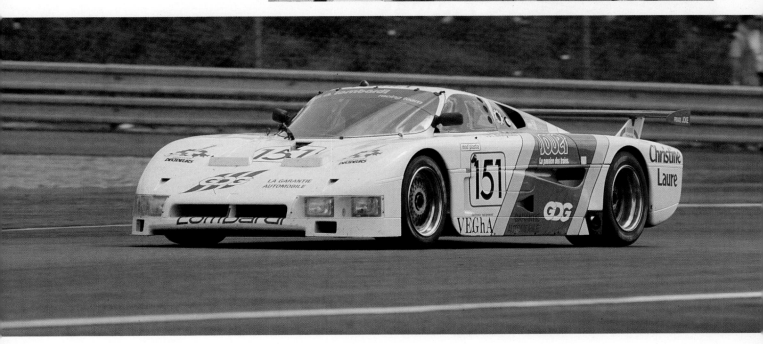

Salazar fifth – both on the same lap as the second placed car in what was becoming a fabulous race to keep up – with Nielsen ninth, the Jones/Daly car only due to last another half-hour before a dropped valve put it out of its misery for good. Nissan were holding on to sixth and twelfth, the remaining places in between filled with the likes of Mass, seventh despite a sidepod damaging spin by Dickens some time earlier, two laps down, then Larrauri, with the Omron car on the move up into tenth just ahead of the black Lloyd 962 and destined to go higher.

*Pierre Yver was another in trouble on Saturday, losing control while trying to make room for the leaders. Although he managed to limp the Primagaz car back to the pits its race was over.*

*Continuing their practice woes, Mazda #203 suffered all manner of problems yet still made it home twelfth overall.*

*The PCGB/Cabin Porsche would either be fast – as here – or fraught, a whole catalogue of problems being overcome before it made it manfully into seventh by Sunday lunchtime. Then. . .*

Further down the order, Schlesser's hopes of glory had finally seemed to have faded with so much time still to run. Electrical horrors meant the Mercedes V8 was unable to give of its best, thereby putting Sauber #62 outside the top twenty down amongst the Aston Martins and also the two C1 Spices. Both of the latter would be out of the race by breakfast.

The GTP Mazdas were going well, the trio split by only a couple of laps. And the Chamberlain Spice #101 still led C2.

By now darkness had all but set in, the long cool night about to begin, a time of pleasure for some and hardship for others. A few would have cause to say later that it was there and then, under cover of darkness, where the race twisted in their favour, many more how it turned against them. As the last vestiges of the pink and purple haze of twilight turned steely grey with the passage of sun and time, did it not signal an omen for Joest or Jaguar? Or were the muted colours of the midsummer night sky heralding the fulfilment of a dream for the men from Hinwil and Unterturkheim?

Only the spirits of tomorrow knew the answer – and there was still two hours of today to run first. Not that the likes of the Lombardi Spice or the Obermaier Porsche were to see the witching hour let alone dawn, three of Brun's five entries also amongst the casualties so far, the ALD another early au revoir.

As the race hurtled towards midnight the fairground was in full swing, the bierkellars and other hostelries packed to overflowing. Everywhere, the avenues and passageways became a mass of drifting humanity, the air they breathed mixed with the smoke from many a culinary enclave, the smell of overdone frites and garlic sausages permeating everything.

Unaffected by such matters, 'Brilliant Bob' was still piling on the pressure in his endeavours to get even further away from those who would deny him a much deserved and long overdue maiden victory here, the gap going out to nearly three laps by the time faraway church bells in old Le Mans town chimed out the turning of Saturday night into Sunday morning. Yet when they tolled for Wollek and Stuck they also rang the

knell of doom for Joest #8 too, the Jelinski/Raphanel/'Winter' Blaupunkt 962 wowing then fluttering before blowing a head gasket just around midnight. And with it plant the first seeds of doubt into the seemingly invincible Joest 'wunder maschine' . . .

*All locked up with no place to go, Gary Brabham brake tests himself on Saturday evening, the Schuppan 962 losing its nosecone against hard Indianapolis barriers moments later.*

*Johnny Dumfries gets to grips with his stricken Toyota, having done his Uri Geller impression with the screwdriver. . .*

*David Leslie sits patiently aboard Aston Martin #19, a steady run spoilt when the engine gave out in the early hours.*

# PROFANITY FAIR

WHEN THOSE valiant men of yore, heroes of the ilk of Magellan and Livingstone, Christopher Columbus and Cap'n Cook, returned home from their travels they would tell wonderful stories of high adventure, recount great feats of danger and derring-do.

When more humble folk speak of Le Mans they also talk in such tones; of having made it through the night without sleep, gotten out to the Mulsanne under cover of darkness, and, most fearsome of all, of having survived a visit to Le Fairground.

So it was that West Yorkshire's answer to Indiana Jones went to investigate some of the lowlights which lay out there in the shadow of the Dunlop Bridge, beyond the twilight zone. . .

It's not really like our idea of a fairground, but is more akin to the American concept of a carnival. And there are not only the usual rides and shooting ranges and so on, but also freak shows, something which has become a rarity back in dear ol' Blighty where sensibilities seem to have put an end to such tasteless displays. Open around the

clock, for as long as the race is on, fairground barkers entice the punters to part with their hard-earned francs for a ride on les bolides, a peek at the fat lady, or to try their hands with the shot-guns. . .

Yes, shotguns. Pushing through the crowded and noisy mayhem of the side-shows, you come across the scene whereby a drunken racegoer, pump action twelve bore at his shoulder, is loosing off at the clay targets, the air full of beer and cordite. Then, he misses one. Merde, alors! In a fit of pique and a barrage of obscenities, he begins to wave the untethered gun in the air, blasting the ceiling of the booth as he does so, a light fitment crashing down at the feet of Madame who gallantly leaps forward and wrenches the weapon from his grasp before any further damage can be done to her property. Or worse. It was all getting kinda dangereuse out there.

Beating a hasty retreat, then there are the rides. Quite expensive and not for the faint-hearted, the G-forces on some of the most dramatic examples rival anything a Group C car car muster. But at least on the Taifun or the Taiga Jet

you should not need to worry about crashing – which is more than can be said of the go-karts, which this year seemed particularly well patronised by the British. Eat your heart out, Derek Bell!

I wonder if 'Dinger' has ever seen a mermaid? There was one at Le Mans – or at least so it said on the outside of the booth. Nathalie, Sirene des Mers, was depicted as we all would like mermaids to be: blonde, buxom and beautiful. In reality she was as leathery as an old boot, not much bigger than the Wellington variety of same, and had been dead for about a hundred years. If, that is, she had ever lived at all. Jack Tar's dreams were never made of this.

Irta, on the other hand, was very much alive – all 244 kilos of her. That translates to 538 lbs or 38 stone; whatever way you put it she's one helluva lady! In the particular seance this intrepid reporter attended, as the curtains drew back to reveal her, one of the spectators (there were three of them, all 'Brits') suggested, in a less than gentlemanly manner, that she should reveal some more of her excessively ample self by –

hrr, hmm – lowering the upper part of her dress, which was only just managing to contain her colossal bosom. Not that he couched the request in such genteel terms either. Her response was a look of pure hatred that would have turned less sturdy nationalities to stone, and despite repeated blandishments the lady's expression changed not one jot, and the flimsy garment stayed firmly in place. Perhaps she did not fully understand the quaint English expression 'G'wun then – show us yer tits.'

As for Erika, the girl who lived with reptiles. . . although the potted palms and bamboo cage did help with the jungle image, the illusion was soon shattered when she shoved one of her lazy snakes aside, and pulled out from under it a packet of ciggies. Many

moons ago, one may never have been alone with a Strand, but the supposedly untamed girl of the wild looked rather incongruous lighting up a Gitanes.

Then there was 'Louisiane', as it said outside one interesting establishment, but whether the girls present actually included a Louise or an Anne was not revealed. Everything else was, and to music, too. But that, as they say, is

**I wonder if 'Dinger' has ever seen a mermaid?**

another story. . .

As is much to do with Le Fairground. Outside again, fighting one's way through the flotsam and jetsam of humanity, the cacophony of the musics accompanying such titillations of the flesh drifted on the still night air, mixing as they did with all the other noises and bright lights which bombarded the senses from all directions. Yet not far away, from just beyond the tree line, came the constant howl of racing cars as if to remind everyone of their presence, Les Vingt Quatre Heures du Mans still continuing apace, the drivers and other team personnel afforded no such distractions.

You could almost be forgiven for wondering as to who was having the most fun. . .

*The sight and sound of 200 mph racing cars is almost lost in the cacaphony of colours and noise emanating from the fairground.*

# A MIDSUMMER NIGHT'S DREAM (Part 2)

IDNIGHT CAME AND midnight went, the Lammers / Gilbert-Scott / Tambay XJR moving ahead of Sauber #61 and into second place as the Frenchman put on a spurt to close the gap on the leader by about five seconds a lap. Fully ten minutes behind the hard charging Joest #9, it would need a long spell of such pressure before the results were likely to show on the leader board. Unless, of course, the pink Porsche hit trouble.

Onwards ever onwards, headlamps like low trajectory tracer bullets under a moonlight sky, the Joest car maintained its routine of fast lappery knowing full well that it alone of the front runners had not lost time unnecessarily. As one o'clock past into history nobody would have bet a pfennig or a centime against Herr Stuck and Monsieur Wollek going all the way to the chequer, the leaders for the last six hours having the pace and the race well under control. Unless, of course, the pink Porsche hit trouble.

Nothing in this great race is as certain as its uncertainty. Avid skiers both, with

Hans-Joachim having taken over from Bob at the top of the hour, suddenly their hopes went downhill, and fast. Only twenty minutes into his latest stint, he was back.

There, in the half-light of the pitlane, Reinhold Joest took on a stoic facade of quiet concentration while alongside him Norbert Singer looked out over half-rim spectacles, his expressive features showing the full anguish of knowing that the chance of great glory might be about to pass them by. A water leak from a small pipe beneath the radiator was causing temperatures to rise and vital life sustaining fluid to boil away, Porsche's chances of victory seeming to evaporate with it. For fifteen minutes the erstwhile leader sat at rest, fifteen minutes in which Tambay was up and away.

As were the #61 and #63 Saubers too. When 'Stucky' finally clambered back aboard to resume his stint at 01H31 it was in the role of chaser rather than the chased, the pink Joest #9 relegated to fourth marginally ahead of two more Jaguars and the Japanese crewed Nis-

san, this soon to be fifth as Andy Wallace moved Silk Cat #2 ahead of the Porsche a few minutes later. The Ferte XJR had lost some more time with exhaust problems but, with all the top seven now covered by under three laps, everyone knew that the race was still very much on, Joest's recent disappointment underlining the fact that there was still plenty of time in which doom and gloom could come a-visiting before a winner would be found.

And having survived many earlier dramas too, nobody knew this better than Sauber Mercedes. While their pole car still languished back around sixteenth, both the other two had been making steady progress up the lap charts, the #61 machine of Acheson and the Italians poised in second, the following Mass / Dickens / Reuter sister car particularly impressive in the cool manner in which it had clawed its way back into contention from such a humbling beginning, now one of the fastest around. Who said they don't come back from beyond?

But second and third are a long way from first and throughout the next few hours those who stayed up to watch the vigil of the night were treated to a truly wonderous sight as everyone chased the front running Jaguar, the pack often separated from each other only by a few seconds as they jostled for supremacy with all the urgency which had gone into those opening laps so many long and tiring hours before. A fusion of lights and colours, only the Japanese Nissan proved unable to keep up the pace in the hours of darkness, a cracked cylinder head just before three o'clock ending an impressive effort which had seen it running as high as fourth.

Onward went the clock and so did the survivors, the tranquillity of a French night broken by the constant roar of raw power, the earth trembling thunder of Aston V8s and wail of Mazda rotary fours most notable amongst them, Mercedes adding their own distinct basso-profundo to the chorus. Wherever you were, be it trackside soaking up the splendours of the occasion or faraway across the fields trying to get some sleep, in the cacaphony that constantly bombarded the senses these three stood distinct above the rest in their tenor.

Whatever the sights and sounds of conflict joined, as the battle raged higher the only thing for sure was that while second through to seventh squabbled amongst themselves, Larrauri bringing up the rear of the front pack, the leader was beginning to open up the gap, the bulletins which greeted half distance showing TWR Jaguar #1 to be one and a half laps ahead of the two Saubers and gradually moving away, it fast becoming a matter of catch us if you can. And nobody looked likely too.

Adding to Jaguar's pleasure, the other two remaining Coventry V12s were coveting fourth and fifth, the solus 'American' Nissan now seventh surrounded by the remnants of Porsche's once mighty assault, a short but spectacular flash fire adding to a night of woe for Wollek and Stuck who had slid back to sixth.

Yet at least they were still going which was more than could be said of Aston Martin #19 when, without warning, David Sears had been left to walk home from the country when his V8 decided it had done enough, thereby bringing a modicum of respite for everybody's eardrums. Meanwhile, despite some interruptions to its lappery, Aston Martin #18 was still battling away noisily further down the order, twenty-third at half time. 'Character building' is what they call it . . .

*Fire! A flash fire while refuelling engulfs the Stuck/Wollek Porsche, Malcolm Bryan's reflex action proving a photographer's art is not always a safe one. . .*

*While the mechanics soldier on, the helmeted Messrs Bellm and Spice take time out to confer with team manager Mick Franklin.*

Just as the opening segment of the race had started badly for the Kidlington equipe, so did the second half of this year's encounter, Michel Ferte bringing Jaguar #4 back in only half way through his sunrise stint, its gearbox in disarray. With the deja vu of previous experiences with one of their number last year, the TWR engineers and mechanics got down to the task of changing the whole rear suspension/transmission despite knowing full well that as a threat to overall honours its race had been run. An hour of hard toil after the rigours of a long sleepless night, nobody who watched them at work relished trading places with any one of the unsung heroes.

Yet no sooner had they finished and sent Michel Ferte on his way again than John Nielsen arrived, a cloud of smoke trailing him in as the harbinger of sad tidings. Secure in fourth place having put their early problems far behind them, the crew of Jaguar #2 had been circulating on the pace and looking good to take on the Saubers when the engine

*'Ballot' climbs aboard his Joest 962 ready for his twenty-third night of Le Mans action.*

*Another night, another pitstop. After climbing doggedly into the top ten dawn would see the engine expire on Lloyd's #15.*

And the Chamberlain Spice still led C2. Taking over twentieth spot where the now defunct Aston had left off, Nick Adams & Co were eleven laps clear of their pursuers, the Argo four ahead of the C2 Cougar Porsche. Baring a miracle for the also-rans and a disaster for Chamberlain, having led the class from the first lap, already the category seemed a forgone conclusion, there having not been a display of such domination hereabouts for many a long day and night.

And day again. As the first inklings of sunrise appeared through the treeline behind the paddock it seemed to symbolise the daylight the first placed Jaguar was continuing to put between itself and all others, Jan Lammers apparently en route to a second consecutive victory, aided and abetted on this occasion by Tambay and the reputation building Gilbert-Scott, 'AGS' admirably filling the role of accomplished rookie which fell so well to Andy Wallace last time around. Ably backed up by their teammates just behind the Saubers, some people were already speaking openly about a possible Jaguar one-two-three.

Yet if there are two things guaranteed about Sunday mornings at Le Mans these past few years, it is that dawn will break and so will the Jaguar challenge. This would be no exception.

suddenly let go, Sunday breakfast therefore bringing with it the unsavoury taste of Jaguar's almost ritualistic cylinder head failure mixing with the bacon and oeufs, the matter manifesting itself with the sad trickle of scalding hot water from a V12 exhaust pipe. It was more a case of belly-up than sunny-side-up for Silk Cut #2 as, bitter with disappointment but nary a backward glance, the TWR guys pushed the car away and got on with the race.

ANDY WALLACE (Jaguar #2): "The whole race started off badly when we got bashed up the rear by the Nissan. After that, we were up to four laps behind at one stage but had pulled it back to only one and still gaining when the engine went on Sunday morning. Up until then I had never given it any thought that we were going to lose. We were on schedule, easy in the fuel, then it went bang. . . ."

*Twenty years after man first landed on the moon, this would be one mechanic's idea of a latter-day Tranquillity Base. . .*

*Dawn at the Esses and a lone survivor of the night charges on.*

Fortunately for them, their spirits were lifted with the knowledge that the Number #1 car was still in the number one position, neither Sauber apparently willing or able to mount any positive attack, it being a matter of just being there less than two laps back, ready to take advantage of any opportunity which may come their way. Indeed, some members of the Swiss/German enterprise were surprised they were so high and had lasted so long, certainly not at this stage of proceedings wanting to chance their luck on any make or break manoeuvre.

As the terraces and tribunes gradually started to fill, their capacity growing with the heat of the morning sun, for sure it was now virtually a race between only these three, the pink Porsche – now

back up into fourth as a result of Jaguar's dramas – requiring increasingly more frequent stops to slake its thirst, each topping up costing vital track time. Behind Stuck and Wollek, Larrauri continued to mount what was tantamount to a one man show in fifth, 'Popi' deserving an Oscar for the way he hauled back the time lost by his slower team-mates, his great run eventually to count for nothing when the engine blew asunder down Mulsanne a few hours later. Often criticised for his Arnoux-like track manners, Larrauri's was one of the great unrewarded drives at Le Mans in '89 but by the time he packed up to go home the whole complexion of the race had changed. And not to Jaguar's advantage.

At just gone a quarter after six, at

06H17 to be precise, Jan Lammers realised that his dreams, those of the team, the sponsors and something akin to a quarter of the overall crowd, were about to disappear along with the morning mist. For four laps he had felt something wrong with the transmission and was now heading in. Derek Daly had suffered damaged selectors while leading on Saturday evening, the Number #4 car a broken third gear when very handily placed just a couple of traumatic hours ago. Now this. As the Dutchman peeled off from the racing line coming out of the Virage Ford and aimed for pitlane, a huge sad sigh went up that could probably be heard back in dear old Blighty, the tiredness factor of the hour now multiplied enormously as defeat stared Jaguar squarely in the face.

*The Mako Spice hits the dust on Sunday morning. It survived.*

*Sunday morning and all is well. Fifteen hours gone and Reuter leads aboard Sauber #63. Note the damaged sidepod.*

As the silent predator sat at bay in its lair, a pool of dark liquid oozed from beneath the left rear corner, team personnel responding to the urgency of the discovery with alarm. The look on Tom Walkinshaw's face told you that it was serious without a word needing to be spoken, the fact that Jan dismounted reaffirming the gravity of the situation. With the back of the car jacked up high in the air soon eager hands were stripping away the whole rear end in a repeat of the exercise so recently carried out on the Number #4 car.

There, in those crucial hours between dark and light, it had all gone wrong for Major Tom and the Purple Army. Not that TWR were yet ready to admit defeat, the Walkinshaw ethic being that the race is not over until the chequered flag falls.

While experts – and others – debated the reasons for Jaguar's sudden downfall with all the earnest concern of politicians and pundits on General Election night, some reckoning it was the failure of a tuppenny-hapenny rubber seal, others 'knowingly' suggesting a new gearbox oil had not been up to the task, all eyes were now focussed on the new leaders – and what leaders they were! Six minutes into Jaguar's latest and greatest calamity, hurtling along past the pits had come a pair of Saubers, their thunderous engines trumpeting a unique fanfare to a very special occasion because, excepting the first few minutes of this year's race, not since the mid fifties had Mercedes led Le Mans!

Seven seconds apart, Jochen Mass heading 'Branca', the sight of those two Silver Arrows in full flight was warming to all but the coldest hearts, their uncluttered coachwork reflecting a magnificent rise from the depths of adversity. They had come here this week with the cloud of last year's very public humiliation still hanging over there heads and despite putting on a good show in Qualifying had gone in to the race worried about the longevity of their transmissions. Now, in an ironic twist of fate, they were the main beneficiaries of gearbox problems afflicting others, the ever spinning wheel of fortune now making victory theirs for the taking.

Not that it was all over yet. Jaguar then Porsche then Jaguar again; they had all led handsomely until suddenly struck down in their prime – and with the Sauber Mercs into the realms of the unknown by virtue of now having lasted much longer than they ever had here before, with best part of ten hours still to run anything could still happen. And, to some, it would.

Including Mauro Baldi. With Stanley Dickens now sitting in for Jochen, quick work at the round of pitstops just before seven o'clock had seen Mauro not only take over from Brancatelli but also grab the lead, his glory lasting only as far as the Dunlop Chicane some minutes later when the brakes failed to rein him in before silver met gold, Sauber #61 spinning helplessly into a sand trap. Able to get out again without undue damage, nevertheless a precautionary pitstop was required and in that time Dickens was long gone.

With all this frenetic activity amongst the front runners, it was easy to overlook the fate of the others, the Almeras 962 having crashed out when twentieth, all three C2 Tigas falling by the wayside earlier on. The trio of C1 Cougars – including the old March Nissan entry – were also hors de combat, a consequence of which being that there would be no 'Local Hero' headlines for Yves Courage this time, unless, of course, his C2 car came good. Not that such a thing looked very likely because, as a distant third in class, whatever else may have happened in the ebb and flow of this topsy-turvy event, one thing remained static and seemed destined to do so for the duration: the Chamberlain Spice #101 still led C2.

*Battle scarred and defiant, the Hydro Aluminium Porsche was the only surviving Brun 962, Huysman/Lacaud/Schaefer making it into tenth by the end.*

*Nobody would begrudge Tim Lee-Davey his Le Mans finish, the gleaming new nosecone hiding a multitude of sins.*

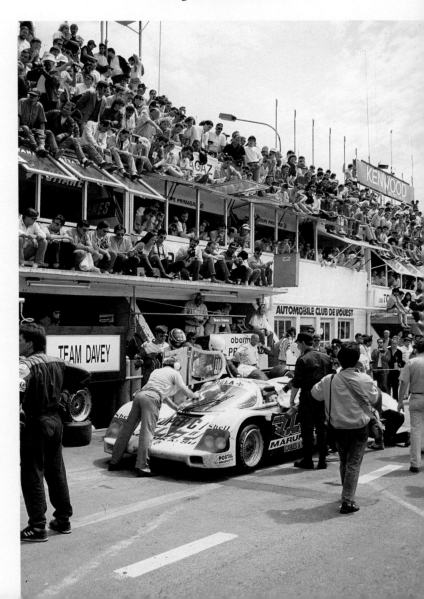

*The kettle's boiling! As Reinhold Joest turns away not wanting to look, the steamy engine of the pink Porsche goes through its Sunday ritual following a cracked water pipe. Anyone for tea?*

The black Lloyd Porsche had also gone, veteran David Hobbs and his young partners having done a fine job hauling the tardy machine into the outer limits of the top ten only for the engine to expire, debutants Hill and Andskar both having acquitted themselves well under the circumstances. As had the C1 Spices, their week wrecked by more calamities than they had probably experienced in a whole season as C2 champions, losing undoubtably coming harder to those used to winning.

Yet failure does not come easy for those who had taken over their mantle and endured seventeen hours of unchallenged supremacy only for their dreams to be shattered in a single sudden moment. At one minute before nine, the sight of Nick Adams cruising the Repsol/Silk Cut SE88C up pitlane took many by surprise, his stint not due to finish for another half-hour. Instead his race was run.

A broken valve was soon diagnosed and although Hugh's crew probed and pondered a long time in the hope of finding some way out of their dilemma it was a lost cause, the suggestion of running the car on seven cylinders not viable despite a cushion of fifteen laps they enjoyed over their class mates. So near yet so far, as everyone gathered around offering comfort and condolences it was indeed a cruel end for such a stirring effort, the team destined to play out their frustrations with the craziest game of rugby ever seen thereabouts, the Pride of Buntingford determined to put disappointment behind them and get on with winning the WSPC C2 crown.

DAMON HILL (Porsche #14): "I enjoyed the whole thing. Driving through the night was brilliant, I managed to get the stints with the sun going down and also coming up, with one in the middle. When you make it through the night you think to yourself that the rest is just a piece of cake. Then the bloody thing went and broke down!"

NICK ADAMS (Spice #101): "It was the most perfect Le Mans run you could imagine. We'd had no unscheduled pit-stops at all, only changing the brake discs because we thought we ought to, it being Le Mans. We were stroking it, about fifteen laps up.

"I was in the car when the engine went. Coming out of Mulsanne Corner they had just come on the radio to remind me exactly how far ahead we were and I remember saying back that I could not go any slower. And as I said it suddenly the power went. I thought it might be a broken manifold as all the temperatures and pressures were fine, and radioed that I was coming in with a problem. I sat in the car for twenty minutes, hoping, but they then diagnosed a dropped valve, and we were out. We had led from lap one for eighteen hours. It was a cruel way to go".

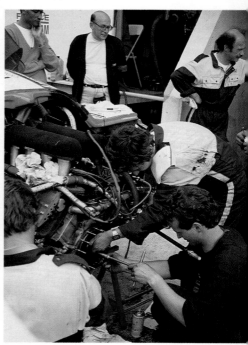

*Meanwhile, the Speedy Argo was unable to take advantage of Chamberlain's plight, their hour long clutch change proving crucial to the outcome of the C2 category.*

*Alone with his thoughts, Hugh Chamberlain ponders the fate of Spice #101 which had led C2 for so long, Nick Adams having just radioed in to tell of the problem which would end their race.*

*Fourth on Sunday morning, gearbox problems six hours from home made the Omron Porsche a last lap special, finally being classified in thirteenth spot.*

Although the news of the hour still showed Chamberlain #101 in the C2 lead, fourteenth overall, the class was now up for grabs. Sadly for them, the Speedy Argo team were in no fit state to take up the offer, their clutch strewn all over pitlane, the Cougar Porsche thereby closing the gap between also-ran and unexpected success. Further back still, the Mako and GPM Spices now also had something more to go for than simply the honour of finishing the race, if, indeed, finishing at Le Mans could ever be described as simple . . .

Up front, Mercedes still led Mercedes, Sauber #63 from Sauber #61 by a full lap, the pink Porsche hanging on gamely in third despite its ongoing saga of regular refills, its position made more tenable by the loss of the 'American' Nissan which had joined the "Liste des Abandons" just before the Chamberlain's Spice when its engine quit. Geoff Brabham had been busy chasing his brother Gary in the Omron Porsche at the time, the Schuppan entered 962 having made an almost unobtrusive rise through the field into fourth position,

the Nissan then fifth. Julian Bailey's early indiscretion apart, as team manager Keith Greene hauled the current IMSA champion out of the mortally wounded R89C, nobody could have failed to have been impressed by the superb showing of the Milton Keynes based Japanese equipe, their showing the best so far for any of the Orientals. 'One day . . .' mused the onlookers. 'Next time . . .' avowed the team.

This time it was looking good for Mercedes, the hours winding down, the opposition getting no nearer, the Silver Arrows closer and closer to a historic triumph with every tick of the clock. Seven hours; six hours; five; as midday loomed large the Saubers thundered on, four laps clear of their pursuers who were led by Wollek and Stuck, Jaguar #1 nine laps further back as it raced to make up the deficit those earlier problems had created, the other surviving XJR even swifter as Alain Ferte set a new outright lap record to underline what could and should have been.

And what, with luck, they hoped might still be. By midday the rise of the

Omron 962 was over, the battered blue beastie having to resign itself to becoming a chequered flag special when the gearbox expired. It would eventually be classified thirteenth. This moved Lammers into fourth but still there would need to be more than just speed if Jaguar #1 was to overcome a leeway of thirteen laps on the leaders. In the last four hours they had made up two, thirteen way beyond their reach in the time remaining.

While keeping up the pressure, Jaguar were banking heavily on the Saubers hitting trouble. The Joest Porsche was wilting quite noticably, its quick bursts getting less frequent, and so was very possibly there for the taking. The Saubers, on the other hand, showed no signs of fatigue despite each lap taking them into previously uncharted territory, especially those supposedly fragile gearboxes. At any time you half expected that Mercedes' magnificent front running display would come to a grinding halt. But, somehow, you guessed that it wouldn't.

*In fifth gear and in flames, Kunimitsu Takahashi has the Kremer 962 hot seat getting warmer by the moment. He was unharmed, the car badly damaged.*

Undeterred and undelayed, as high noon came and went so the two front running Saubers continued to circulate the thirteen kilometres of history, their third car now having made it into a respectable fifth spot. Porsche were having to use ingenious methods to keep going – including the pouring of "Coca-Cola" over the clutch to dissipate some oil – while Jaguar were still chasing their rainbow in the hope of finding a miracle.

Standing beneath a hot naked sun in a cloudless sky, the Purple Army knew in their hearts it was not about to happen, the race realistically all over bar the shouting. And even that was more muted this time, last year's overwhelming scenes not being repeated as the chance of victory drifted slowly away. They would cheer each pitstop, wave banners as each lap was completed, but it wasn't the same . . .

All over bar the shouting. For some maybe but not for others, certainly not the Kremer brothers. Just a few minutes into the afternoon session, Kunimitsu Takahashi came past the pits in fifth gear and also in flames, his fiercely burning Kenwood 962 finally coming to rest in the Dunlop Curve gravel bed. Tenth at the time, one minute ahead of the Ferte Jaguar, it was a sad way to go out, the little Japanese driver given a warm – but not too warm! – ovation by the crowd as he walked back in to recount his adventure to Erwin and Manfred. If they did not have bad luck, they wouldn't have any luck at all.

Nor would Richard Lloyd who, after having seen his PCGB/Cabin 962GTi struggle to a respectable seventh, then had it repeat the 'Taka' treatment two hours later, Tiff Needell at the wheel. Two years ago, on their last outing to Le Mans, RLR had also gone home with an overcooked wreck as their main souvenir of a week's unrewarded hard toil. Today would be no different. A faulty batch of fuel pipes were reckoned to be the cause infernale of both conflagrations.

And for similar reasons a finish would also be denied WM on their last ever outing at Le Mans, the stop-start-stop again run of the much troubled jolly green giant finally terminated at 12H30 when, out around Indianapolis, it too caught fire thereby bringing a Viking end to a brave Gallic story. Never again will their like be seen in The Great Race, their passing a sad but defiant one. Au revoir, mes amis!

TIFF NEEDELL (Porsche #14): "The tank was full but we knew something funny was going on because the fuel pressure kept flickering. So I was having a sniff around and keeping an eye on the mirrors when, just as I was passing the entrance to pitlane, I saw a plume of smoke. It was a good job I did not bring it in otherwise there would have been a pitlane full of flames. I just parked it and got out."

*Tiff Needell suffered the same fate as 'Taka' two hours later. Note the guy in red shorts atop the wall of the ACO building. . .*

If somebody had said "well done" to personnel from any of those teams at that moment they would probably have risked physical assault. For very different reasons, the possibility was the same in the Sauber Mercedes pits as the race entered its final phase, such was the intensity of emotions thereabouts as what was once counted in hours now became a matter of minutes, nobody wanting to celebrate too soon. Just in case.

The nearer they got, the higher went the anticipation, the sweltering heat of the day reflecting off those acres of stark concrete only adding to the explosiveness of the situation. And when Kenny Acheson brought the second placed car in after only a single lap of his final stint, with less than ninety minutes to run, if someone had blinked, let alone burped, then the whole place might well have ignited. As everyone held their breath in an atmosphere so charged you could almost touch it, suddenly the men in the blue and white faced the possibility of having victory pulled from their grasp at the last, Sauber #61 suffering from the much dreaded gear selection problems.

For six long minutes the team busied themselves around the rear of the car before declaring there was nothing to be done other than press on. Acheson hit the starter button, the engine fired, the dirty silver racer moved forward – and stopped. Only able to use fifth gear, the car had stalled. Firing it up again, slipping what remained of the clutch, at the second attempt slowly man and machine edged forward and away.

The fear was that whatever had struck Acheson may also blight the leader too, the reduced pace of a now unchallenged run to the flag no guarantee against disaster, a delay of only fifteen minutes more than enough to turn glorious victory in to galling defeat. In those moments, the hopes of Porsche and Jaguar must have risen, the cold sweat of Sauber Mercedes taken on oceanic proportions. Could it be that we were in for more late drama than any Hollywood epic? Could it be that there was still further twists to come in this incident packed race? They were tense times at Hinwil-sur-Sarthe.

KENNY ACHESON (Sauber #61): "Second place wasn't bad for my first race at Le Mans, the one-two-five result being more than the team hoped for at the beginning, for sure. In twenty or thirty years I think it will probably be looked upon as an even greater result than it is now.

"Even if we had not had the gearbox problems towards the end I do not think we could have caught them. Both cars could run at about the same speed so unless they had a problem we were never going to make up the deficit. And we were too exhausted, both physically and

mentally, to catch them even if such a thing was possible.

"Driving the car stuck in fifth gear was easy – I only had two pedals to work! All I had to do was use the mixture switch; richen it up in the corners and lean it back on the straights. The engine has that much torque. I did not know if we could finish and did not want to come in again for fuel because we did not think we could get out again in fifth gear. But after about fifteen minutes they came on the radio to say the fuel was okay and after that it was just a matter of keeping going."

*Sitting and waiting and hoping and praying. Sauber mechanics wait out those last laps ready for anything.*

*Tensions ran high for Sauber when Kenny Acheson needed gear linkage repairs less than two hours from hime, All ended well.*

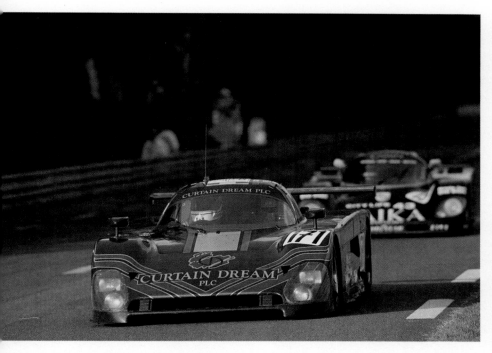

*The final round-up. With twenty minutes to go Sauber #63 stops for a quick slash'n'dash.*

*It would be a dream come true for the Mako Spice C2 of Hyett/Shead/Sterling with a fine second in class.*

*Heading for victory. Jochen leads his team-mates and an interloping pink Porsche through the Virage Ford for the final time, the sweet relief of success now only moments away.*

With moments taking on the agonising proportion of millenia, Jochen Mass' arrival for his scheduled pitstop a few minutes later ended the agony as swiftly as it had started, the sight and sound of his healthy machine reassuring team personnel that all was well with Sauber #63. When all was said and done they breathed a cumulative sigh of relief and sent him on his way.

Porsche would have to make do with third, Jaguar not bettering fourth, both teams acutely aware of how they both had thrown away golden opportunities to win by virtue of those time consuming delays. As a result the tortoise was about to beat a whole host of hares. Porsche would have the consolation of unexpectedly picking up C2, Jaguar a new lap record, but it was not the same, not by a long way.

Mazda would show them all how to get cars to the finish, all three GTP screamers making the top twelve overall, Aston Martin astonishing themselves as much as anybody by making eleventh, cheered on by the Purple Army as if they had won. In their own way they had. The Hydro Aluminium 962 went one better with the last of Brun's once proud equipe, another splendid against-the-odds effort. And nobody would begrudge Tim Lee Davey getting through the twenty-four hours, his team so underfunded they find shoestrings expensive let alone kamikaze co-drivers.

Whatever the ifs and buts and might have beens, here and now the race was all about Sauber Mercedes and Jochen Mass. When the popular German hero completed a quick 'splash and dash' fuel stop with only twenty-five minutes to go even the likes of Peter Sauber and his team chiefs Max Welti and Dave Price afforded themselves a quiet smile, there being nothing left for them really to do but await the inevitability of the outcome. By now their pit was a mecca for all and sundry, Hawaiian Tropic girls and Gitanes belles mixing with cameramen and journos, sponsors and hangers-on as everyone jostled to be in the centre of the action come the finish.

All around the track, the flags that had waved for Jaguar and others were now uniting for the good men of Hinwil, their small and enthusiastic team still made up ostensibly of many a part-timer, their open friendliness a credit to all they represent. Nobody would begrudge a win for the good guys.

The last few minutes were counting down and the excitement going up. By the time Jochen came around to start his last lap he had caught the lumbering Acheson and with Jabouille also getting in on the act the three 'Silber Afriel' lined themselves up in arrowhead formation ready for a photo finish, all cameras and eyes now seeing only them. Around they went again, the clock on the pitwall clicking resolutely on to the appointed hour as they did so, the crowd already invading the track before they returned.

Up in the Sauber pits it was bedlam. Mechanics were singing and sponsors were dancing, Peter Sauber and Max Welti standing on the pitwall hoping to get a glimpse of their charges as they came home across the finishing line. They never made it, the swarming masses blocking the path of the victors not far beyond the Virage Ford, Jochen and Kenny and Jean-Pierre unable to get any further. Hoisted high by the fans, Sauber had won, Mercedes had won, it was hail to the conquering heroes, hurrah for the three pointed star! Peter hugged Max and Max hugged Peter, nobody else probably able to comprehend the relief and fullfilment they felt after the traumas of last year.

It may not have been revenge but it was still as sweet. As was the champagne that was now going high in the air, the revelries already in full swing. Soon joined on the wall by Mercedes motorsport supremo Jochen Neerspach and technical wizard Hermann Heireth, the four men stood there as the crowd gathered round, hardly able to believe their good fortune, something each and every one of them would have found highly unlikely last evening.

Theirs had been a long night but a winning won. While it is said that only losers feel tired, no doubt after celebrating with their kith and kin, friends and supporters, eventually this momentous and historic weekend would come to an end. Then, each one of the heroes who had fought so hard, be they driver or engineer, mechanic or tyreman, would eventually drift off to their beds unwilling to sleep yet unable to avoid the inevitability of it.

*To sleep perchance to dream.*
*To dream the dreams of the magnificent.*

BRIAN REDMAN (Aston Martin #18): "I think it did amazingly well to finish. We were off the pace but not by much. There were a few minor problems but in only its second race it's about as good a result as we could have hoped for. The engine actually gave more power at the end than at the beginning, with little leak-by, and was in perfect condition – so we are going to petition the Le Mans organisers to make it forty-eight hours next year!

"My most notable memory of the whole affair was when the suspension broke at full speed down Mulsanne on Sunday morning! That apart, with only a couple of hours to go I had been sliding it quite a bit around Arnage and a group of gentlemen on the right were jumping up and down quite a bit waving and shouting so I waved back at them. Then on one lap I did not slide it and next time round they held up a hand-written sign saying 'Give Us More Oppo'. The time after that I nearly spun it! Then they held out a sign requesting 'Now, Fastest Lap'. Finally, they put out one saying 'Crumpets and Tea with The Queen'. It was a bit of light relief . . ."

*Max Welti, Jochen Neerpasch, Hermann Heireth and Peter Sauber;*
*the architects of victory.*

KEITH GREENE (Nissan #23/24/25) : "It was disappointing not to finish at least one out of the three cars, the last one being at 0830 on Sunday morning with the 'American' car. We think it was the scavenge pump.

"On the 'Japanese' car it was, to some degree, their own fault. In England we had moved the oil cooler by making a different mounting from the one Lola supplied. We told the Japanese about it but they decided not to follow us, so when the oil cooler moved across hitting a clip on the water rail, as we suspected it might, and caused a leak. Then they did not respond quick enough to telemetry signals telling them the water temperature had gone up, I don't think, and when they came in someone put stone cold water into the engine without even starting it up. It split the cylinder head.

As for the 'British' car, it was not Julian's fault. In fact he could not stop, our brakes being nowhere as good as those of the Jaguar. If you look at the video it clearly shows he was about thirty yards behind Nielsen where they dog-leg slightly right at Mulsanne Corner, and he just caught him up. It was as if Nielsen had given him a brake test. He didn't but that was what it was like. 'Jules' braked harder and harder and harder until the rears locked up, put some opposite (lock) on, and still could not stop, the angle of his front wheel pushing the wishbone into the tub. That was rain-stopped-play after only five laps. It was not – as everyone thought it was – a young Formula One hero trying to be smart-arsed . . ."

TOM WALKINSHAW (Jaguar #1/2/3/4): "How would I sum up Le Mans '89 for us? Terrible! Our preparation for the race was as near perfect as you could get but we ran into problems that we had never experienced before, tracking it down to a components supplier. I'm fairly confident it won't happen again.

"As regards to whether Mercedes won it or we lost it, I do not think there is any question that both ourselves and Porsche lost the race. There were only two teams who went there with cars fast enough to win it based on the experiences of the year before. Porsche knew how fast they had to go and so did we. Mercedes were not capable of doing so and, as far as I can see, just ran their cars to finish the race. But the leading cars had problems and they inherited the win. However, any way you win counts and you cannot take anything away from them. At the end of the day they did a good job and won the motor race . . ."

MAX WELTI (Sauber #61/62/63): "We did not get to celebrate much as there was a race only a fortnight later at Jarama. There was no big fiesta.

"We had suffered a lot of problems last year but what everybody forgets is that we were there for two years before that and we learnt quite a bit then. When things went wrong last year, everybody thought 'Oh, these bloody Swiss bankers, they're a small team, not enough money; now they have to learn for another three years'. Nobody believed us – especially some journalists – when we said that we had prepared properly, but we had. We had done a lot of testing.

"This year's victory is still unbelievable because I never expected it. The first time I thought we had a chance of winning was just before the start of the last lap! I was convinced that at least one of our three cars was good enough to finish in a good position but would not have reckoned on first place. There really was a question mark over the gearbox but we had an idea to improve it on Friday so that is what we did and in the end it showed to be quite okay. We improved it by changing quite a bit inside. . .

"Maybe we had some luck the others did not have but you have to have some to win. It is fantastic, very important for the team, really fantastic."

# ALL'S WELL THAT ENDS WELL

IT WAS a glorious evening, without a cloud in the sky, yet up at Pit 17 the air was full of thunder.

Dave Prewitt was overseeing his Spice C2 which sat forlornly on pit road and was not a happy man. Only five hours into the twenty-four, the GP Motorsport SE87C – Yellow #108 – looked to have rolled the dice and lost, another early pack-up-and-go-home on the cards for the small Silverstone equipe with the big hearts. Last year, with this very same car, they had led every race they entered only to suffer problems, Le Mans being no exception. Then they had managed to stay around until gone midnight. Today, it was still barely nine o'clock . . .

A persistent misfire was proving untraceable, the consensus of experience and opinion narrowing the probabilities down to it being the sensor mounted up front on the Cosworth DFL, the same item which had heralded their demise when well in command at Silverstone a year ago. Twenty-eight laps down on the class leading Chamberlain car already by dint of earlier spark box problems, the fact of the matter was that it is a two hour job to get to the suspect component and reassemble everything afterwards, not the kind of task to be undertaken lightly in the overcrowded anarchy of the Le Mans pit lane as darkness loomed upon them. Nor were there any guarantees of success.

"I am not going to retire it this time like we did last year" said the determined and stocky Midlander, the memories of having battled against a spate of wheel bearing failures last year only to have their efforts evaporate into oblivion when the clutch gave out, still fresh in his mind.

"If we had got stuck in to that clutch we could have finished third in class. So I am not going to retire this time without giving it our best shot. There is still a long way to go."

Yesterday had been his daughter's 21st birthday and this was no way to celebrate. Indeed, the week had been one drama after another, the list of disasters which had befallen GPM already reading like a catalogue of auto racing calamities.

During only their second lap of practice, Evan Clements had felt the V8 tighten as he sped down Mulsanne. Thinking it was a dropped valve he backed off. It wasn't a valve but a piston, number seven to be precise. Exit one engine.

With their race unit installed as a replacement, GPM got the Spice out again just before eleven o'clock that night only for the lights to fail on the same driver as he approached the notorious Mulsanne Kink at full speed on his Qualifying lap! Not something to be recommended, in the half dark Evan could just about see his way clear without lifting, the time good enough for fifty-second place on the overnight grid.

This became forty-ninth after Thursday's efforts, courtesy of Dudley Wood, despite a coming together with Ricci's

962 as the Joest Porsche returned to the track from a pit stop. Such was the damage inflicted in that moment of mayhem – a broken nose, cracked undertrays, shattered wheel and a puncture – that he took fifteen minutes to make it back around for repairs. Once again the hard pressed GPM mechanics would be more than usually busy during the lull between the evening's two sessions.

And so the saga continued. With the car once again refettled but the handling way off beam, it was a final straw when the oil pressure dropped as regular driver Philippe de Henning sped down Mulsanne some time later, early fears of another terminal engine problem allayed when the team later discovered a faulty cockpit guage to be the culprit rather than the V8 itself. It was the best news they'd heard all week!

*Dave Prewitt was not a happy man when engine problems looked likely to terminate Yellow 108's race after only five hours.*

*For a while it looked as if 'Pedal' might be the only option open to the drivers but it all came good in the end. Note the tools above Roy Baker's right shoulder!*

They had come with high hopes and continually seen them dashed, the list of difficulties encountered enough to deter all but the strongest of wills. But motor racing is nothing if not a breeding ground for optimism: "Hopefully all of our problems are behind us" said Dave Prewitt on Friday afternoon. But you somehow got the impression it would indeed be another eventful outing for the GPM Spice . . .

And you would not have been wrong. The race had hardly gotten past its first thirty minutes when Dudley Wood slowed going past Les Hunaudieres, crawling round to the welcome sanctuary of pitlane. Off came the back and while routine maintenance items such as tyres were attended to there was also the more serious matter of having to change the sparkbox.

Less than two hours later, it happened again, de Henning left stranded on the circuit out by Indianapolis for forty minutes while he fitted the on-board spare. By the time he got back to Pit 17 that too had failed.

Every pitstop seemed to bring fresh drama, the 3.3 litre DFL unable to run cleanly for more than a trice, the problem eventually traced to be a broken rotor arm in the distributor.

"I think my little car has a gremlin in it" muttered Prewitt, the lustre of his canary yellow shirt not reflected in the blackness of his mood. A persistent misfire had not been cured by the new rotor arm, the mystery deepening as minutes ticked on by as willing hands sought to solve this latest woe.

Testing this and tightening that, pushing and pulling, looking and wondering, nobody seemed able to find an instant answer to their woes, the race continuing apace without them. Time was moving on and so were the leaders, Spice #108 now a full two hours of track time down on the Chamberlain car which led the way for the C2 field, Nick Adams & Co yet to miss a beat.

If it was not one thing then it must be another, slowly and methodically the team began going through their check lists in a vain attempt to find the answer, nothing effecting a cure, their investigations not made any easier by the fact that in the pitlane Yellow #108 was not being subjected to the same stresses she endured out in the heat of battle, the symptoms not repeating themselves while the car remained at rest.

But, by the process of elimination, it just *had* to be the crankshaft sensor, buried as it was deep in the motor where the forward face of the mighty V8 meets the rear chassis bulkhead by the amidships fuel tank. To get to it would mean removing the whole of the car's rear end, not in a race shop but amidst the crowded chaos of a darkening pit-lane.

"I am not going to retire it this time like we did last year" reiterated the team chief.

As the crew prepared themselves for the seemingly inevitable, suddenly there came a stroke of good fortune. The crankshaft sensor joins the sparkbox at the same place as does the cable from the tachometer – and disconnection of the latter had appeared to effect a cure. Could it be that some internal fault with the rev-counter was 'spiking' the whole electronic system? Would it be the answer to all their woes?

Hastily reassembled, the mood now one not of exasperated despair but

guarded optimism, everyone had their fingers crossed as team manager Roy Baker stood ahead of the pulsating projectile ready to give the signal to go once everything was ready to do so, the sign board in his hand which simply said 'PEDAL' being the last recourse open to GPM if all else failed. With a harsh metallic clunk Evan Clements selected first gear from the non-syncromeshed transmission and, waved on his way as much in hope as farewell, edged forward into the sunset, all the assembled GPM entourage hoping not to see either car or driver again for quite some time.

Less than four minutes later he was back, not in the pits but blazing past half empty grandstands, chasing the beam of his headlamps, all appearing and sounding well. Then again, and again. At last it seemed as if the tide was turning for Dave Prewitt and friends although they knew only to well that a problem cured is a problem ready to reappear again without warning, every passing of their charge a bonus on what could have been, each lap they now completed edging them closer to fulfilling their dreams of finishing the race. Forty-fourth overall, eleventh in class ahead of only the much delayed and soon to depart ALD, Tiga #105 and ADA, their's was a mountain to climb. But as someone had once remarked, even the longest journey begins with a single step . . .

Over the next few hours each of the drivers took their turns trying to haul Yellow #108 back into some form of contention, midnight seeing them having gained six places overall but only one in class, the Lombardi Spice joining some silent big guns in early retirement. But as Saturday night turned in to Sunday morning, this soon became ninth when Chamberlain's turbo car decided it had done enough and was packed off early to bed.

*The GPM Spice C2 fought long and hard for its eventual third in class.*

For the good men and true of GP Motorsport, onwards ever onwards went the race, their constant vigil under the dim lights of pitlane straining every nerve and sinew as they willed their machine around one more time, one more time, one more time . . .

Some laps were lost when the clutch needed a couple of lengthy stops for attention, ten in total, but as the sun rose out of the Manceaux sky shortly after half distance, the reward for their endeavours was thirty-first overall and seventh in C2, the 'works' Tiga and France Prototeam's Spice now behind them. The fact that Chamberlain's rapidly reliable Cosworth car was a whopping forty-three laps ahead mattered little, they were never going to catch it, so what the heck. What was more important to GPM was the fate of the Mako Spice and the sole surviving Porto Kaleo Tiga, both of whom could be caught if things swung in their favour.

Constant lap after constant lap, Yellow #108 continued to circulate on schedule, each passing hour raising hopes which looked so close to being cruelly dashed in the fading light of the previous evening. Pitstops came and pitstops went, everyone now running on adrenelin and bloody-mindedness, the long cool tiring night having given way to a long hot tiring day, each and every one of the team members afraid to make the error which might cost them so dearly, one slip now all that was needed to undo everything that they had come so far to achieve.

Seventeen hours down with seven to go, as the smell of breakfast drifted across from the terraces suddenly a buzz went up the pitlane that Chamberlain were in trouble, their fifteen lap advantage on the C2 field of only academic value as the stricken machine sat receiving attention. Although it would be quite some time before Spice #101

would be wheeled away, in that dropping of a valve the whole C2 roadshow had moved on.

Not that the Speedy Argo – then second in class – was capable of taking advantage of the situation, its clutch already strewn all over the pitlane a couple of bays up, the delay long enough to deny it any moment of glory. Indeed, it would be another hour before the Cougar Porsche finally inherited a lead it would never lose. To finish first, first you have to finish . . .

The crew of Yellow #108 knew this only too well and were happy to find themselves up to fourth in class, the GPM machine going better than it had all week, the final Tiga having also fallen by the wayside, the Graff Spice much delayed. Meanwhile, the Mako SE88C remained only four tantilizing laps out of reach and about to move ahead of the Argo.

## They were going to 'gently Bentley' it

Twenty hours gone, four still to be done, the GPM Spice was now within a couple of tours of the Argo, the gap widening to three in the next sixty minutes, then down again soon after as fortunes ebbed and flowed.

"I'm told the Argo has gone on to seven cylinders" said Prewitt with only 2½ hours left to run, the sense of urgency in his voice embodying an unspoken new optimism: "You don't wish anybody bad luck but a finish in the top three would justify the boys' efforts."

Almost imperceptibly, the mood was beginning to change chez GPM. On the Friday, driver Clements had stated as to how they were going to 'gently Bentley it' in an endeavour to get home in one

piece but now, with a possible third place in sight, the whole operation went up a notch. What was, for so long, a feat of endurance, was now, at last, becoming a race.

As the event entered its final two hours, the Speedy machine was still a lap and a bit to the good, the gap as small as it had ever been but realistically impossible to close in the time available, GPM willing to roll the dice but not to stake their all on a third-or-bust finale. All they could do is keep the pressure on and hope the Argo would hit more problems.

There was just over an hour and a half left when they got the break they needed. At precisely 14.28 journalist Rousselot brought the stricken machine in to tell a tale of woe regarding the electrics and that is where it stayed for thirteen vitally unlucky minutes, time in which the GPM Spice was up and away.

Winding down the last stints, GPM came home a mere nine laps behind the class winning Cougar, despite having been 'off piste' for over three hours of the duration, still four shy of Mako. Seventeenth overall; in the first half of the race Yellow #108 had managed only 132 laps, the second portion recording 171, the disparity of the numbers thereby telling the story of their fortunes. Yet whatever the ifs and buts of a C2 defeat ripped from the jaws of possible victory, more than anything they were relieved to have made it to the chequer.

Third in class was a bonus, the big reward for GP Motorsport being simply to have finished. With the way things had looked at nine o'clock the previous evening, that in itself was victory enough.

*The GPM data board, a diary of triumph over adversity.*

# TWELFTH KNIGHT

*'AGS' with Patrick Tambay and the Ferte brothers. Did he have a frog in his throat?*

**A** FORMER Formula Ford Festival winner; a past Grovewood Award recipient; the current British F3000 championship leader; although Andrew Gilbert-Scott has some worthy credentials to his double-barrelled name, there were a few raised eyebrows when it was mentioned amongst the dozen who would defend Jaguar's honour at Le Mans this time around.

Yet despite the added pressures of it being his Jaguar debut and also his first ever visit to Les Vingt Quatre Heures du Mans in any capacity, their scepticism proved foundless, 'AGS' doing an excellent job in helping the Number #1 car to fourth place after gearbox problems thwarted a possible victory. Shortly after the event he spoke of his adventures:

"As a new driver, when you first go to a team you sometimes feel that nobody is going to be bothered with you. They weren't like that at all. They could not have been more helpful.

"And that includes my team-mates Jan Lammers and Patrick Tambay too. The icing on the cake was to be in the Number #1 car with them and they were superb, one of the reasons I managed to do as well as I did. I'd only done about one hour of testing before Le Mans and only ever raced a F3000 on the 'Bugatti' circuit there. I had not even seen the Mulsanne! A lot of what I would otherwise have had to find out for myself – don't do this, be careful of that – they had already told me about. They could have just wandered off . . ."

Yet talking with the established stars can only help so much. Eventually he would have to experience it for himself:

"Alistair McQueen, the engineer on our car, is a good friend of mine, having known him ever since I first got involved in motor racing as a mechanic working on Fernando Ribiero's Formula Ford. I had said to him that the one thing I did not want to do was to have to learn Le Mans in the wet and the dark. But, of course, it poured with rain on Wednesday and I had to go out in the second session. It was a bit spooky, the fog coming down as well, but the car was fantastic. They told me just to do a few laps to learn the track a bit and tomorrow, on Thursday, if it was dry, I would have a chance to 'drive' it. Which I did – and I got straight down to a 3m30s. Something like that".

In an arena not known for modesty, false or otherwise, the ACO timekeepers actually clocked him at 3m29.13s, some way off team leader Lammers, but also nearly two seconds better than Tambay.

"As for the race itself, we worked out a good race strategy and it was looking good. We were leading all through the night and if we had not had that problem I'm sure we would have won it. We were on our fuel, looking very strong, and had not even really started to race. It was a great shame because the cars actually had the pace whereas last year I think they were slightly lucky in some ways. But this year they were really the quickest cars out there."

And he was thrown in at the deep end when things went wrong on Sunday morning:

"I was the first one in the car after the gearbox had been changed. We were 17th or something ridiculous at that stage, and they told me to be 'slightly' careful – which was a bit nerve racking – as the boys had been working for hours and were very tired and had just bolted a whole new rear end on."

That there were no further problems is a credit to the skilled dedication of the TWR staff, the fact that the car made it home fourth only a 'mere' nine laps down on the winners despite losing an extra hour of track time a clear indication of what so easily might have been. Nonetheless, 'AGS' remains very philosophical about how things eventually turned out:

"Some people try for years to win it and, in many ways, if I had done so at my first attempt it makes it almost too difficult to go back and repeat it. Fourth is great, I can build on that . . ."

# MUCH ADO ABOUT NOTHING (ACT I)

**G**ERMAN/English dictionary – Sauber [zow'berr] ; a. clean, tidy, pretty Zauber [tsow'berr] : n. charm, spell, magic

KNOWN TO everybody as 'Chip', his real name is not Edward G. – as with the famous movie gangster – but Edward C. Robinson, native of 'Noo Joisey'. IMSA GTP champion two years ago, he holds the record for the fastest qualifying speed in American road race history with a lap of 143.99 mph at Watkins Glen in July of 1987, driving a Holbert Porsche 962. Disagree, and he will probably fill your chassis full of lead!

HENRI Pescarolo and Claude Ballot-Lena each started their twenty-third Le Mans this time around. Coming into the race, the combined number of starts for the whole of the Jaguar pack was a mere twenty-five!

HANS STUCK is known in the Joest press information as 'Strietzel'- a word in Bavarian slang for which there is no known direct translation into English. Maybe that is why the ACO's media guide refers to him as being Danish . . .

MAX BOSTROM, designer of the Aston Martin, was previously responsible for the unremarkable F3 Nemo built in Ireland back in 1970. Not a long c.v., begorrah.

IF THE managers of three British based WSPC teams had bothered to respond to messages repeatedly left to contact your humble scribe, one of them could have had the chance to employ a top name NASCAR ace with a spare weekend. And the chances are that besides adding a lot of skill, colour and interest to their efforts, he may well have brought some sponsorship along too. Don't ring us, we won't ring you . . .

THERE WERE lots of Weissach engineers 'vacationing' at Le Mans: Walter Naher with Brun, Norbert Singer at Joest, Roland Kussmaul at Kremer and Klaus Bischoff taking time out with Kremer. Of the top Porsche runners, only Richard Lloyd's team were omitted from such assistance, Stuttgart being markedly unsupportive of the highly individualistic efforts of the small Silverstone equipe. A case of being non-user unfriendly?

ACCORDING TO information received, Stanley Dickens is distantly related to world renowned novelist Charles.

THE ACO advises that there were 230,000 spectators attending the race this year, a 15% increase on 1988. They also state that there were 2,030 accredited journalists/photographers from thirty-one countries as well as crews representing twenty-eight different television channels. And they must all have been in the pitlane together, seeing as how crowded it was!

ACCORDING to the team, the silver of the winning Sauber is the same shade as that found on the Swiss postbuses.

ROGER SILMAN, team chief of TWR, and Will Hoy, under-rated sports car racer, are brothers-in-law by virtue of being married to sisters. What a pity Jaguar did not keep it in the family and give him a run in a XJR9LM.

MANUEL REUTER has long been noted for a colourful array of helmets, the mirrors off his winning Mercedes of a very similar hue. Could this be the start of a trend?

COSTAS LOS of Aston Martin was an early contender for the 'Quote of the Week' award with his line : "If we can finish that would be very good because the top fifteen cars that finish are usually in the top fifteen". It's all Greek to me!

THE C2 ADA lost its driver's door twice in quick succession because new springs on the catches resonated open, such are the vibrations inflicted by the 13 kms track. Earlier, at scrutineering, the car was found to be a mere one millimetre too wide. While everyone else sheltered from the second hailstorm of the day, team members could be seen braving the elements tightening it all up to the organisers' eventual satisfaction. Or did it shrink?

THERE WERE only two WSPC races prior to Le Mans this time, at Suzuka then Dijon, both venues new to the WSPC. Their combined total distance of 960 kms represented less than one third of the build up available for La Sarthe twelve months ago, the total then being 3160 kms. Nor was there the traditional Test Weekend either. All in all, it was not the ideal way to prepare for a marathon equal to a whole season of Grand Prix racing . . .

THERE CAN be few racing drivers who have a brother in an alternative occupation which is considered more fraught than his own. While one of James Weaver's kith and kin is a more sedate accountant, the other serves as 'Our Man in Afghanistan' to the Washington Post. Brave chap!

THE WISE men of Weissach could be deemed as instrumental in their own downfall. About one-third of all research and development done by Porsche AG is for outside contracts, Mercedes having entrusted them with vital racing components some time ago. They did the job well, perhaps too well!

ONLY FIVE cars started on Michelins: the WM which caught fire, the Cougar-Porsche which won C2 and the three Saubers. . . .

SAUBER team manager Max Welti would like to compete in the Spa 24 Hours as a driver. The 1980 Swiss National champion, his only appearance in such a capacity at Le Mans ended abruptly when John Nielsen took unscheduled flying lessons in the Sauber C8 they were to share with Dieter Quester in 1985.

CHAMBERLAIN Engineering were able to run Silk Cut logos on the C2 Spice C2 of Nick Adams, Fermin Velez Bisbe and Gigi Taverna as the Gallaher/Jaguar contract guarantees exclusivity only for WSPC rounds, something Le Mans wasn't. For a while there it looked like a win double . . .

WE BRING you the information other books cannot reach! Ian Hutchinson, the clever man who has styled the liveries for all the Silk Cut Jaguars and much more besides, advises that the XJR purple which has caused sleepless nights for many a modeller is officially Pantone 259. He also says that when viewed from a three-quarters front angle, the looped orange portions above the headlamps are symbolised cat's ears. So now you know!

RICHARD LLOYD'S bright red Cabin Porsche started the race with its PCGB decals missing from above the right-side headlamps, the mistake only being rectified at the third pit stop. That'll put the modellers into a dilemma!

ANDREW Gilbert-Scott, who celebrated his 31st birthday on the day the race started, is the grandson of the founder of the Morgan Car Company. Could that be the reason his XJR9LM was sometimes less a ferocious feline, more a misbehaving moggie?

TWR ALWAYS have an impressive array of support vehicles at race meetings, amongst them being the ubiquitous motorhome. This particular example contains a room at one end – all pale grey upholstery and pink slatted blinds – into which Mr Walkinshaw apparently takes anyone in need of a lashing from that raw Scottish tongue, a daunting prospect indeed. Legend has it that recipients of such action have been seen to crawl back out under the door without needing to open it first! It could be politely known as "Uncle Tom's Cabin". However, it is more succinctly referred to as "Tom's Bollocking Room" . . .

HUGH CHAMBERLAIN wins the 'Quote of The Week' award with his Saturday morning rendering of: "Thursday was perfectly all right, the intention being to get everyone qualified for Day and Night. Except that it was Wednesday – which goes to show I know nothing at all! But I know it exceptionally well!".

# A TALE OF TWO STICKERS

**M**ODEL-MAKERS tend to take a great interest in even the tiniest details of racing cars so anyone planning to do the yellow and blue Hydro Aluminium Brun Porsche 962 number 16 will have noticed that between practice and the race it acquired two extra stickers atop the doors. The decals simply say 'MacAllister', and there's a story behind them . . .

Chris MacAllister is an American car enthusiast who owns some rare gems, including a beautifully restored Ford GT40. We first met back in 1986, at Mid-Ohio racetrack, when he was running the car in a Shelby American gathering at the Lexington venue. Since then, having recently read my book on Porsche 956/962s, he decided that one of Stuttgart's finest would make an ideal stable-mate for the Ford; the best of the 'Sixties, plus the best of the 'Eighties. Only a 917 would then be needed to fill the gap . . .

So it was that he telephoned me last January, asking if I could try and find him a suitable Porsche. Intrigued at such a fascinating prospect I immediately set about my quest, 'phoning here, there and everywhere, eventually arranging a meeting between him and Brun Motorsport's Peter Reinisch to take place in a Florida hotel just prior to the Sunbank 24 of Daytona.

And there, under a blazing sub-tropical winter's sun a deal was quickly struck, thereby making Chris the proud owner of Porsche chassis-number 962 128, the 'Torno' IMSA car which was in the process of being converted to Group C specification for this year's 24 Heures du Mans.

Many enthusiasts own ex-Le Mans cars, a few even saw their cars race there years before they ever came to own them, but Chris was now in a rare and envious position whereby he could go to France to see the car in action, knowing that it was his. He could share in the worries, the excitement, and (hopefully) the joys of a Le Mans 24 hours, in a way denied to virtually every other classic car owner. It would be a rare treat.

Not long before the race he learned that his car was to be sponsored by Hydro Aluminium, a large multi-national metallurgical company based in Norway. Their blue and yellow markings had not been overly inspiring when viewed at the Nurburgring last year but now, styled with flair and eye-catching imagination, Le Mans '89 would be a different story, the car one of the most striking on parade.

"I guess the first thing I was concerned about was what the car looked like in the Hydro Aluminum livery" he said upon arrival, first practice about to begin: "The contrast between the colours is very pleasing, and the geometric design very impressive.

"This is my first visit to Le Mans, something I have been planning to do for ten years now, never before having a good excuse to make the trip" he continued, looking down on the pristine 962, his pristine 962, which lay at our feet before adding the inevitable rejoinder: "And this is the best excuse I can think of!"

Chris plans to try to keep it as original as possible, in its longtail Le Mans trim. "I am considering taking delivery exactly as it leaves the track, with the nicks and everything. We'll just have to see how badly it's beat up. It will be especially memorable to have the car in future years, and to have been there when it was raced, and to know the full history of this particular race; it really is a very big plus that none of my other cars have. It will be something special."

And for someone so enraptured with the car and the whole event, he was therefore surprisingly calm as the car first made its way out on to the circuit. Whereas many amongst us might be horrified at the thought of our latest mega-buck classic crumpled against armco, or worse, Chris had confidence in the driver line-up of Uwe Schaefer, Dominique Lacaud and Harold Huysman – notwithstanding that the latter had never raced at Le Mans before.

*Chris MacAllister and the Brun Motorsport Hydro Aluminium 962. His other car is a GT40. . .*

*The way the new owner wants to remember his car.*

"These guys are professionals, and I expect them to drive fast, and not to do anything stupid, but I don't want the car to come in twentieth place. It has to be competitive, otherwise it's not the essence of the sport."

MacAllister's Hydro Aluminium 962 would eventually start from twenty-seventh spot, half way down the massive Le Mans grid.

"It was interesting to talk to Harald Huysman; he went out the second session, when it was dark, raining, the track was wet. And here's a guy out in my car who has never been on Le Mans before! It was a terrible time to send him out for his first drive – at least they coulda given him a road car to go round the track a coupla times, but no . . . ! I asked him about it afterwards, and he said, 'No problem, I learn circuits fairly quickly', so I was somewhat relieved . . ."

Although the 962's colour scheme had been all worked out, with every decal placed 'just so', Chris pestered Peter Reinisch until – on race morning – he conceded that the car could also wear a couple of decals of MacAllister Machinery, the Indiana-based family company which sells caterpillar tractors, and of which Chris is a Vice-President. After all 'cats' are rugged pieces of machinery, and maybe the MacAllister decals just might bring the Brun Porsche a bit of nine-lives luck . . .

Having been instrumental in making the Brun/MacAllister connection, I too felt particularly interested in the fate of old '128, and it's surprising just how much I worried when the car had an unscheduled stop, and how relieved I felt whenever it got going again. Le Mans is notoriously hard on cars, and the new owner was naturally hoping that the gods would smile on #16, and allow it last out the race distance. If it could manage a top ten finish, well, wouldn't that be something!

There would be problems with electricals and puncture damage to attend to but by 4pm on Sunday, having spent the whole 24 hours in the pits, Chris was still there, together with his wife Sharon, straining to see over the heads of the crowd as #16 reeled off her final laps to take the chequered flag. 962 128, sole survivor of the five Brun Porsches, had made it to the end, a dream fulfilled. And in tenth place at that!

Returning to the Americas soon afterwards, Chris MacAllister would have quite some story to tell the guys back home. I wonder if his road car carries a sticker saying 'my other car is a Porsche 962' . . .?

# LOVE'S LABOURS LOST

## The Man . . .

"**I** HAVE HAD IT about six years but have only managed to find enough time to get the engine out and stripped down. One day I'll finish the restoration and go to Le Mans in it!".

Graham Humphrys was talking about his first love, a Citroen Traction Avante. Going on to explain how the 'Maigret' car was good looking, ahead of its time and oozing character, he could just as easily have been describing the Spice prototypes he has been designing since the company started in 1985 – because what with being amongst the prettiest competitors around the sportscar racing scene these days, their 3.5 litre of normally aspirated C1 challenger is leading the World Sports Prototype Championship into the brave new world of 1991.

Quietly spoken and unassuming, this son of a former motorcycle racer from Nuneaton first got involved with automotive design as an apprentice at Jaguar back in 1967, his seven full years there coinciding with such landmark roadsters as the new XJ6, the first V12 E-type and the XJS.

They were, as he readily admits, great times to be at Browns Lane, working alongside many of the old crew who had brought the Coventry marque such glory a decade and more earlier, but eventually he started to look around for a new challenge, a magazine advertisement leading him to Hesketh Racing. Teamed with Harvey Postlethwaite in the somewhat surrealistic world of the 14th Baron's self indulgence, there was plenty of fun to be had by all though Graham is quick to point out that life at stately Easton Neston was not just the one long round of hedonistic pleasures many people imagined:

"It was hard work, very hard work, we did a lot of all-nighters' he says without false bravado, before adding that seemingly inevitable rejoinder: 'But there were quite a few parties too!''.

Indeed there were, including the one at their favourite hostelry immediately after flying back from James Hunt's dramatic victory in the 1975 Dutch Grand Prix. It ended with His Lordship leaving the winner's trophy propped up behind the bar. But that, as they say, is another story. . .

Yet nothing lasts forever, the end already nigh for Hesketh's Heroes, and when it all went flat at the end of that year Humphrys joined Aston Martin, working out the chassis and suspension for their strangely styled Lagonda then spending much of thereafter developing his theme. There was also the more than tempting prospect of an Aston Martin Group 6 racer for Le Mans, plans of which, alas, did not get much further than the first outlines on his drawing board:

"It was going to be driven by Ray Mallock and Mike Salmon. I actually started to map things out but it did not get very far before being scrapped''.

Cancellation of that project was probably the last straw, five years at Newport Pagnell enough. It was time to move on again.

Setting up as a freelance, the early Eighties were spent on all manner of programmes including the Unipart Ensign F.I. then, after their amalgamation with Theodore, Teddys Yip's IndyCar scheme. In the end both were beaten by money andpolitics as much as anything else, neither realising the potential Graham suspects they had.

Another valued client was March Engineering. Brought in to design a Sports 2000 racer, he was also on call when Robin Herd planned his first tentative forays into the lucrative IndyCar scene. He also penned the 'lobster claw' March 82G sports car, a forerunner of the Porsche powered device which ultimately won the 1984 Daytona 24 Hours.

Away from Bicester there was also the Nimrod. In between his other assignments, Humphrys had been working closely with Ray Mallock to modify the car from its original design in an attempt to make the recalcitrant beast more competitive. There would be much talk of doing a brand new Aston V8 powered Group C car.

But by then Graham's whole perspective had moved on apace, although not before utilising the Nimrod lines in a cut'n'shut operation over his newly designed monocoque to become the neat little Ecosse which eventually took the 1986 C2 Teams title from under the noses of Messrs Spice and Bellm. They would have to content themselves with a shared Drivers' crown.

Having also been involved making changes to 'Gordy' and Ray's Tiga, he obviously impressed the team enough to be asked to join them when they elected to break away from running other people's hardware and start making their own, managing director Jeff Hazell simply telling Graham to 'stop messing about' and join them in Spice Engineering. He took the hint. That was in early 1985. The rest, as they say, is history.

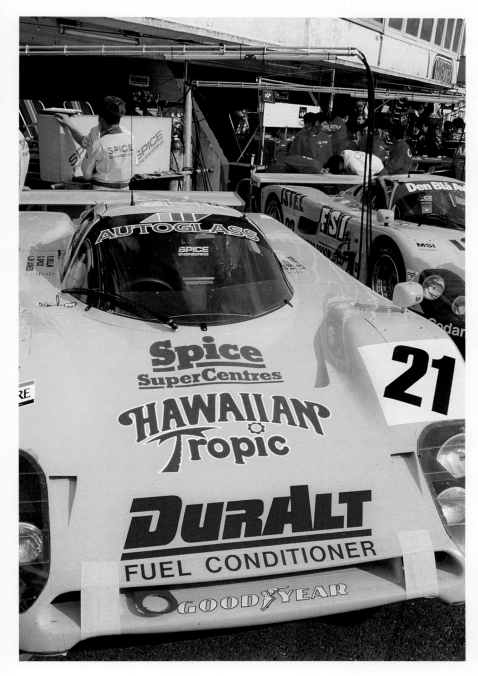

## It's evolution rather than revolution

## The Machines. . .

TWO TEAMS' and three Drivers' titles later, Spice Engineering notched up eighteen victories in only three seasons of C2 – including all but four of their last twenty WSPC races, two of which were at Le Mans – before moving up a gear to C1 for 1989.

Now in a pond surrounded by bigger fish, nonetheless the company has been the focus of an inordinate amount of interest this year because their method of doing so has not been to take the conventional route of the present incumbents but go racing with the first of the new generation, their atmospheric 3.5 litres with its unlimited fuel allowance marking the first moves by anyone towards what will be *de rigueur* for them all in the WSPC as from the opening salvoes of the 1991 season.

Yet a lot of people are under the misapprehension that this year's Spice C1 is simply a big-brother copy of the C2 model which won virtually everything these past few seasons. Very similar to what has gone before in many ways, nothing could be further from the truth, although the old adage that the more things change the more they stay the same was never more apt:

"Many people have looked at the C1 and groaned that it is just a grown-up C2 and while that may be the case in certain respects, it is, effectively, an all new car. Wider and longer than last year's C2, the body is new, the suspension changed, the rear geometry revised, the brakes larger, the engine tipped at a greater angle. There is a new gearbox with a longer bellhousing.

"The original car, debuted back in 1986, was always designed to accomodate C1 power so part of our success was to produce a car that had been over-engineered for C2. The front uprights are still the same castings as used on every single Spice built to date while the basic monocoque design is also common to all our cars. It's straightforward, rugged and has done the job. It's evolution rather than revolution".

Designed from the outset with 700 bhp in mind, to date there have been a total of thirty cars built by Spice Engineering, the final pre-Le Mans one being despatched to Martino Finotto in America just prior to the team setting off for La Sarthe, its Ferrari power unit typifying the fact that whereas many people consider all of the company's products to be much of a muchness they could not be more wrong, variety definitely being the spice of this particular life:

"There have been eleven engine installations, five body shapes, five brake packages and four or five gearboxes. We have a detailed specification sheet for each individual car thereby enabling our customer spares people to give the correct parts to the various teams. When there are clashing dates we can have over two dozen cars all racing at the same time!".

## The Problems. . .

NINE OF THEM were racing at Le Mans, seven in C2 plus the factory's pair of new C1 runners. A lot of speculation has followed since FISA announced the new rules as to whether or not the new breed of C1 cars would be capable of lasting the distance at Le Mans, such thoughts actually leading one ACO official to comment that to ensure someone was around at the finish, rather than open entries up for cars each with three drivers they may have to make it a driver with three cars!

And with neither of the C1 Spices seeing the chequered flag this year, it gave more food for thought regarding the problems of preparing a car specifically for the rigours of the French marathon. Having won and lost at Le Mans, Graham Humphrys knows the requirements of victory there better than most and started his dissertation on the subject by talking of the whole new challenge which has come his way this season with the new Spice C1 cars before broadening his train of thought to consider those faced by everyone who attempts to tame Le Mans and its mighty Mulsanne.

And the fact of the matter is that a designer is really a structural engineer and making a racing car which will give a good account of itself at Le Mans, on the washboard tracks of some IMSA street circuits, or wherever, is akin to trying to put up a skyscraper on quicksand in an earthquake zone:

"The first thing you must take into account is that the 3.5 litre DFZ develops considerably more power than the 3.3 DFL we used in C2, with far higher rpm. In C2 we used to run at 8,500 rpm, maybe 9,000 in Qualifying, whereas now we are between 10/11,000 rpm for long periods".

More power, with higher revs, inevitably leads to increased vibrations, the 3.5 litre more of a shaker than the 3.3, all of Cosworth's V8 masterpieces with their flat-plane crankshafts renowned for similar idiocyncrasies:

'Suddenly, all manner of components started to fail. We've had exhausts crack, the starter system disintegrate, the smallest of brackets fatigue; items which have been on the previous cars for YEARS without any problems, simply breaking because we have changed the magnitude and frequency of the vibrations they now have to endure with the new engine package'.

This year only one-third of those who started the race were still running by its conclusion, many of them having spent a long time changing/repairing failed components. Only the winners can really claim to have had a relatively trouble free run, thereby giving lustre to the adage whereby to finish first, first you must finish. Any of the next four could have won but for technical hitches, a

**Running down there flat out at high rpm and high loading, any component which gets excited and hits its frequency along the Mulsanne can be history, by the time it gets to the other end!**

story of 'if only' which can be repeated right down through the order.

Looking deeper, only one from a total of fifteen cars entered in the last four Le Mans events by TWR Jaguar has raced through competitively without major drama – and it won! The others have suffered what seems to be a never ending spate of damaged transmissions and/or engine failures, often on Sunday morning.

Likewise, when one delves into the 'works' Porsche 956/962s around which such an aura of invincibility has grown up, on their debut there in 1982 the factory team were not pushed hard as the opposition wilted around them, while a year later neither of the pair which staged that dramatic close finish could have survived another lap. Missing 1984 completely for political reasons, they were comprehensively beaten by their own privateers the next time around, while for both of their other triumphs, 1986/7, the car which came home to glory was the only survivor from teams of three. Last year they suffered broken water rails and it proved crucial, this year's 'quasi-works' Joest #9 being afflicted by a similar race-losing calamity.

So why is it that top teams with big budgets cannot build something which

will last the distance now, let alone in the supposedly 'fragile' era which awaits us? Graham Humphrys throws some interesting observations into the picture:

"Le Mans is unique. Intense preparation is essential but there is no way of really preparing for it at all. Testing will give you some information – you can find cracks and prevent some things from breaking as a result of it – but there is no substitute for racing and racing miles. Nor are the shorter races much of a help when it comes to Le Mans because until you have done the mileage you never know if you are pushing something beyond its limits – and we did 16½ hours at Le Mans which is beyond all the racing we had done prior to that.

"A team can have a problem one year and try to resolve it by modifying the car. They then go testing, taking the revised components to Silverstone or Paul Ricard, or wherever, and everything seems okay. Yet when they get to Le Mans it is the same old story.

"And just because a car will break a bracket at Daytona there is nothing to say it will snap the same one at Le Mans, or vice versa. The engines vibrate at different frequencies, the tracks induce different loadings.

"Nor is it a case of simply beefing up certain items, rubber mounting or isolating specific components. It's design, it's development. It's so easy to add weight to prevent a failure but if it is not done with care all you will do is make a weakness elsewhere further down the line. In fact you could be aggravating a problem by putting more weight on to an already weakened component. You don't always get it right first time, often solving one problem to create another elsewhere.

"The only way to test for Le Mans is at Le Mans – especially with regards to the Mulsanne. Nowhere else can you duplicate the same corners, the same entry speed onto that six kilometres of straight, the same bumps, etcetera. No other track has that sustained rpm you get along the Mulsanne. Running down there flat out at high rpm and high loading, any component which gets excited and hits its frequency along the Mulsanne can be history by the time it gets to the other end!".

History will recall that in their first venture to the Sarthe as C1 contenders, the good men and true of Spice Engineering came and saw but did not conquer. Older and wiser and more experienced in the ways of this particular world, they will return again next year even more determined to put on a strong account of themselves.

By then, perhaps Graham Humphrys will have finally gotten around to restoring his old Citroen in order to drive it down to Le Mans.

And maybe he could return home a winner. . . .

# MUCH ADO ABOUT NOTHING (ACT II)

**M**ERCEDES first used the three-pointed star back in 1909 to symbolise their desire for supremacy on land, at sea and in the air. Nowadays the modern Daimler Benz group only use the logo for their automotive activities despite owning such diversities as the AEG electronics firm, Deutsche Aerospace and the recently acquired MBB which includes Messerschmitt. Could that be a prelude to a 700 bhp Me109e Le Mans 'bubble' car. . . ?

DAVID HOBBS – who logged his twentieth participation at Le Mans since debuting in 1962 aboard a Lotus Elite – was 50 years old on the Friday before the race. Someone reaching his own half-century on the day the event finished was John Not-So-Young Stewart, the triple former F.1. World Champion who only raced at Le Mans once, sharing the Rover BRM turbine car to tenth place with Graham Hill in 1965.

WHERE WAS the first ever 24 Hours motor race? Le Mans? Never. Daytona? No chance. It began on 2nd July 1905 at Columbus in Ohio, the Soules brothers' covering 828½ miles in their Pope Toledo. Two years later a pair of such events were run within six weeks of each other near Philadelphia closely followed by no less than three in the New York area that same summer.

A NOTED Japanese company of model makers recently introduced a superb 1/24th scale kit of a 1966 Le Mans-winning Ford MkII. The information sheet with it gives its inspiration not as Eric Broadley's fabulous Lola GT, as was the case, but something known as the 'Roller GT'. Ha so, a crewe-d mistake, methinks. . .

THIS YEAR marks the tenth anniversary of Klaus Ludwig's first win at La Sarthe, the other two coming aboard Reinhold Joest's famous yellow #7 in 1984 and again a year later. Teamed with him aboard the Kremer Porsche 935 a decade ago were American brothers Don and Bill Whittington. Whatever became of them?

The answer is that in 1986 they were arrested for smuggling marijuana into Florida. Allied to money laundering and tax evasion charges, both pleaded guilty on all counts. Amongst their assets seized and confiscated by the authorities was the Road Atlanta race track in Georgia and the Le Mans winning car,

this being valued at a cool US$203,350. In all the brothers forfeited US$7 Million!

Don – whose real name is actually Reginald – was the lesser of the two evils and released from prison after eighteen months, William being required to serve one-third of his 15-years sentence before being eligible for possible parole.

In November '88, Don – sorry, Reginald – apparently drove up to a bank in Delaware asking to cash in the contents of his car's trunk. No ordinary car boot sale this, it amounted to no less than one hundred one-kilogram gold bars!

It appears that when listing their assets prior to seizure, the brothers

somehow 'forgot' to mention their bullion stash, this being, so the rumours go, less than half the amount they were believed by the authorities to still have in their possession.

The bank, as is routine for large bullion transactions, reported the incident to the Federal government who immediately instructed them to issue the payment cheque not to Whittington but themselves. It came to US$1,322,212. The authorities say that if the former race ace tries to claim the money all the relevent agencies will file a case against him; if he does not, the money will go towards reducing the National Debt. Watch this space. . .

# THE ODYSSEY

WINNING AT Le Mans comes at the end of a long, hard road. Not just the three thousand miles or more of this very special weekend but years of graft and toil. We take a peek at the careers of those who got to stand atop the podium this time and discover how they came to be there:

### Jean-Claude Andruet:

European Champion of 1970, Andruet also counts winning the 1972 Tour de France, 1973 Monte Carlo and 1977 San Remo high in his long list of rallying achievements. In 1977 he also won the Spa 24 Hours. He has competed nineteen times at Le Mans in everything from an Alpine-Renault via Ferrari 312P and Lancia LC2 to WM Peugeot, his best overall placings being fifth in 1972 (Ferrari Daytona) then again eight years ago (512BB). He is 49 years old.

### Stanley Dickens:

Hailing from Sweden, the 37-years old Dickens was European Sports 2000 champion back in 1981. After that things went somewhat quiet before he re-emerged as one of the quickest men of C2, winning two rounds for Gebhardt in 1986. Since then he has mainly divided his time between Japan and Joest, winning the All Japan Sports Prototype title last year (with Hideki Okada) and also notching third place at Le Mans. This year was his fourth race start at La Sarthe.

*Pierre Dieudonne and David Kennedy had seen it all before, but for Chris Hodgetts a Le Mans class win was a whole new experience.*

*Looking remarkably fresh, the three winning drivers seem as if they would rather go around for another twenty-four hours rather than face any questions!*

### Pierre Dieudonne:

Now in his twentieth season of motor racing, Pierre has now recorded his third straight IMSA class win at Le Mans, his fourth in total, having competed there eight times. The 1976 European Touring Car co-champion, he has won the famous Spa 24 Hours three times plus numerous other European/World saloon car races. 42-years old, he is a Belgian motoring journalist.

### Phillippe Farjon:

Making a comeback after a decade away from the sport, Farjon started rallying in the early sixties, winning various regional events over the next twelve years. First raced at Le Mans in 1964, his Rene Bonnet aerodjet netting twenty-third. He competed there a further three times over the next eight years, all in Porsches, without success. Now into his forties, 1989 would be his finest hour . . .

### Chris Hodgetts:

A former Birmingham milkman, Chris started racing ten years ago, mainly in national sportscars. Won his class in the British saloon Car championship in 1985, the outright title in 1986 and again in 1987, driving a Toyota. Third in C2 on his Le Mans debut last year, aboard the Tiga Porsche.

### Shunji Kasuya:

A 27-year old economics graduate of Wako University (yes, really!), Kasuya started with karts before moving into the Fuji Freshman series aboard a Mazda RX–7, winning his class in 1983. The following year he was runner-up in a Nissan. Since then has mixed his saloon commitments with some F3 outings. Finished eleventh in the All-Japan 1000 Kms race at Fuji in April, driving a Mazda 757. Le Mans was his first overseas venture . . .

### David Kennedy:

Someone else scoring his third consecutive Le Mans IMSA class win, David almost made it into Grands Prix, failing to qualify the awful 1980 Shadow on all seven attempts he tried. A very frequent Formula Ford winner, notching two top British titles in 1976, he was also a regular front runner in 'Aurora' F1 before the abortive move into GPs. Since then has mainly raced in Japan. His seventh Le Mans, the red-headed Irishman is thirty-six years old.

### Manuel Reuter:

A winner in only his second Le Mans, Reuter is another former karter and made his big wheeled debut in 1983, winning the German FF2000 title the following season. Although he has also raced F3 and sportscars, his most notable success in recent seasons has been in saloons. Until now. Runner-up in the German series two years ago, today he drives for the factory supported Mercedes team of one Jochen Mass . . .

# FAR FROM THE MADDING CROWD

"I HAVE NOT done any television interviews on the strength of it. Not one" declared Jochen Mass, his magnificent triumph at Le Mans already more than a month old. "Reaction to the win in Germany was mainly about it being the Silver Arrows, more on the make than the drivers. That's okay. It is supposed to be like that."

Not for Jochen the megawatt media attention that followed Emerson Fittipaldi's win at the Indianapolis 500 a few weeks earlier. Whereas some would have expected a ticker-tape welcome and at least a short red carpet as public recognition of their success, he was content to play down the importance of the event and his part in the scheme of things, a wry smile emanating from behind those warm blue eyes as he shrugs:

"It is nice to have won it but . . ."

Nor for him the 'Medallion Man' approach to life, the 42-year old knowing there is a lot to life beyond the chequered flag. And as one of the 'winningest' men in sportscar racing

ever, with 105 Grand Epreuves also to his name, he is not only respected throughout motor sport for his achievements but also as one of the pleasantest and less conceited drivers around, his feet firmly on terra firma – despite having a great passion for boats and, more recently, hot air ballooning!

"You have to get up really early, but it is worth it. Some mornings are just *unbelievable*. Really. High up, three or four thousand metres, so called mountains are just little bumps. It's magnificent". Far from the madding crowd, the noise and hassle of the world's race tracks, although he recounts with obvious pleasure the excitement of having crossed Australia from coast-to-coast in an event organised as part of that country's Bicentennial celebrations last year, much of this activity takes place over the the African savannah, having recently gotten involved in a wildlife reserve close by the famous Kruger Park, his wife, Esti, hailing from Cape Town, their two sons, Innes and Quen-

tin, still at school there.

A noble and sincere man, a shade of 'green' before it ever became chic and fashionable:

"We have a lodge built in the trees already. On our Earth we have less and less wilderness available and South Africa is one of the few countries recognising the need to preserve it for the future. It's quite fascinating. I believe there is a great need for people to be able to go and see it and get the spirit of the wilderness which will otherwise become extinct, an Earth without wilderness being a very depressing place."

The Nullabor Plain or the High Veldt, it is all a long way from the dreams of a seventeen year old son of Munich who was lured from his home by the call of the ocean. That was in 1965.

"I joined the merchant marine for three years before starting racing" is how he describes the launching of his love affair with the sea. "I started out as a deck hand and graduated through the

ranks to become an able seaman. I wanted to become an officer or a captain eventually, but quit before getting anywhere near that when my racing ambitions took over."

Well known for his unassuming laid-back attitude whereby it is only the next race which counts, the publicly stated limit of his ambition not encompassing anything so narrow minded as titles or championships, his reasons for getting into the sport underline the free spirit of the quiet man in the blue and white helmet.

"It is the individual freedom of motor racing that appealed to me most. When you get in to a race car, although you are, in many senses, trapped, you are also free. It is you who drives the machine, you who are master of your own destiny. It is the same with balloons or sailing.

"I am not a speed fanatic; speed is relative" he confirms. "You have to take account of winds and tides or thermals, it is an exacting science. If you are in a

hot air balloon and want to land somewhere, suddenly it all gets to be very fast. It's the same with a boat. Perhaps you are only going at seven or eight knots, ten maybe, but you can get dizzy with the speed!"

Nonetheless, the Alfa Romeo GTA with which he started racing was decidedly quicker than that and, showing early promise in a season and a bit of saloon car racing, the young Jochen Mass was taken aboard by Ford as a contracted driver for 1970, some outings in Super Vees soon giving way to hillclimbs and Formula Three before moving swiftly into F2, a win at the Nurburgring two years later topping a season which had also seen him take the Spa 24 Hours (with Hans Stuck) aboard one of those mighty Cologne Capris en route to clinching the 1972 European Touring Car Championship drivers' title.

"They may have been spectacular to watch – but they were also spectacular to drive, too!" he recalls with obvious relish. "They were quite a handful. Not easy to drive, but good fun!"

Two wins against the BMW tide the next year helped net second place in the European F2 series, Jochen also making a very brief Grand Prix debut for Surtees before Jody Scheckter did his infamous 'rock ape' act at Silverstone, decimating the grid in one swift manoeuvre. A second attempt at Watkins Glen three months later ended in engine failure just after half distance, but at least with the satisfaction of having gone further than either of the other two TS14s that overcast autumn afternoon.

By the time the F.1. parade passed through upstate New York twelve months later Jochen had defected from Team Surtees to an upbeat McLaren, his four season tenure at Colnbrook bringing a win at the 1975 Spanish GP and second place in Sweden two seasons later amongst a stock of twenty-three finishes in the points and two fastest laps. He was also well on course to win at the Nurburgring in 1976 if it had not been for Niki Lauda's fiery and famous accident stopping the race.

Then there was talk of joining an emergent Frank Williams: "but it never materialised."

Eventually he wound up at ATS under the autocratic Gunther Schmidt, head of today's Rial F.1. equipe.

"It was absolutely disastrous, an absolute nightmare" is how Herr Mass sums up a wasted twelve months. Thirteen events, ten starts, no points; it was

probably a blessing in disguise when a testing accident ended his season early, a broken left leg less painful than his all ATS experiences thus far.

"The years with Arrows were not bad, I quite enjoyed them" is today's assessment of 1979/80, his quietly spoken manner belying the turmoil of those such as the notorious A2.

After a year's sabbatical, Jochen Mass' F.1. career ended in the spectator enclosure at Le Castellet, half way through a season with the RAM March team of current WSPC overlord John MacDonald. With such an horrendous accident coming so soon after his innocent involvement in that of Gilles Villeneuve at Zolder, it was the last straw. Nobody thought any the worse of Jochen Mass when he turned his back on Grands Prix forever.

He had achieved much but there could have been more, a fact he readily admits, especially with regards to the chasing of top drives. "I was a bit lazy in that sense. I certainly did not play my cards right on leaving McLaren", the suggestion being that he was not ruthless enough in the hurly-burly 'me, me, me' game of Grand Prix musical chairs, the answer coming quietly, without remorse or rancour: "Yes, that's right. I was too relaxed. I cannot regret it because that is the way I am."

Unlike Jacky Ickx: "It was almost sad when he stopped after ten years; never the same again. It was almost like being married. Almost! Sometimes he tended to use his team-mates a little bit for his own ends, was slightly on the selfish side. most people are, I suppose . . ."

Although Jochen had previously won the 1975 Enna 1000 kms in an Alfa T33 alongside Arturo Merzario, it was his decade alongside the Belgian which sticks in the memory, the pair winning together on a record sixteen occasions upto and including Jacky's farewell race, at Shah Alam in 1985. Yet by that time their Le Mans scorecards, the only ones which really matters in many people's eyes, reads Ickx six and Mass none.

To this day still unhappy about many of the safety aspects and overblown 'hype' he says surrounds it, Jochen often chose to miss Le Mans, 1989's successful foray marking only his ninth participation in the last eighteen events. He had debuted back in 1972, the Cologne Capri he was sharing with 'Stucky' blowing its engine during the night.

"When I have done Le Mans I have always done it wholeheartedly – but I am not an enthusiastic Le Mans competitor" said the 1986 pole position man. "I opted out and Jacky became a hero. But I was often quicker than him . . ."

And less lucky. You could almost guarantee that if any of the ultra-reliable 'works' Porsches broke then it would be the one showing 'J.MASS' alongside a little Deutsche flag painted on the door, his second place in 1982 being the only decent finish he could record there before now. The same ofter applied elsewhere too, the Mass misfortune often a major factor in not accruing more wins and accolades to his name.

When victory finally came at La Sarthe this June, it was Jochen's twenty-second ever success in 'world championship' type sports car racing, four IMSA wins – including the 1987 Sebring 12 Hours – also marking the card of Group C's top pointscorer, bar none. Second in the WSPC title chase in 1984, third a year later, what a pity there was no such recognition for the drivers back in those heady days of the mid/late seventies. What a pity that Le Mans this year did not count triple points as it had done last. . .

The person probably least worried about it all is Jochen himself, especially when he is up and away in his hot air balloon or off into the wide blue yonder aboard his ship. A full 120' three-masted schooner, with it he plies the seven seas, once again master of his own destiny, having finally made it to being a ship's captain. Crewed by four or five – six on Trans-Atlantic crossings – the 'Aquila Marina' has been home from home everywhere from the Americas to the Med, the Caribbean to Sweden.

"I never wanted to have one for myself" he explains modestly: "but wanted to support old ships to keep them alive". Currently undergoing restoration in Portugal, when finished she will operate out of Maputo (formerly Lourenco Marques), sailing the Indian Ocean as far as the Archipelago des Comores. Combined with the ballooning and the wildlife reserve, although there are tentative plans to do some CART Indycar racing – he has already tested a Quaker State Porsche at both Weissach and Le Castellet – Jochen sees his longterm future in this idyll, opening up a wider vision of the world to those who choose to see, people with a similar sympathys to his own.

In a press handout at Le Mans this year, various members of the Sauber Mercedes team detailed their favourite films, music, food and so on. Another question asked as to who they most admired in motorsport. To a man, everyone nominated Alain Prost, Ron Dennis and/or Niki Lauda – except Jochen Mass, who chose Mike Hailwood. The former motorcycle ace had been a contemporary of Jochen's at Surtees where they soon became firm friends, Mike the Bike's sad death in a road accident a few years ago robbing motor sport of one of its finest ambassadors.

"He was, to me, one of the best human beings in motor sport. A good guy, a great guy, he was good fun. Straight. Extremely talented, quite a character. He let people live, never 'imposing' himself on anybody although you could always feel his presence. He was a somebody. He had a big heart and was not selfish at all, caring a lot about other people without making a fuss over it."

Jochen Mass said that about Mike Hailwood. Anyone who knows him would say the same about Jochen Mass.

*Close up of a winner.*

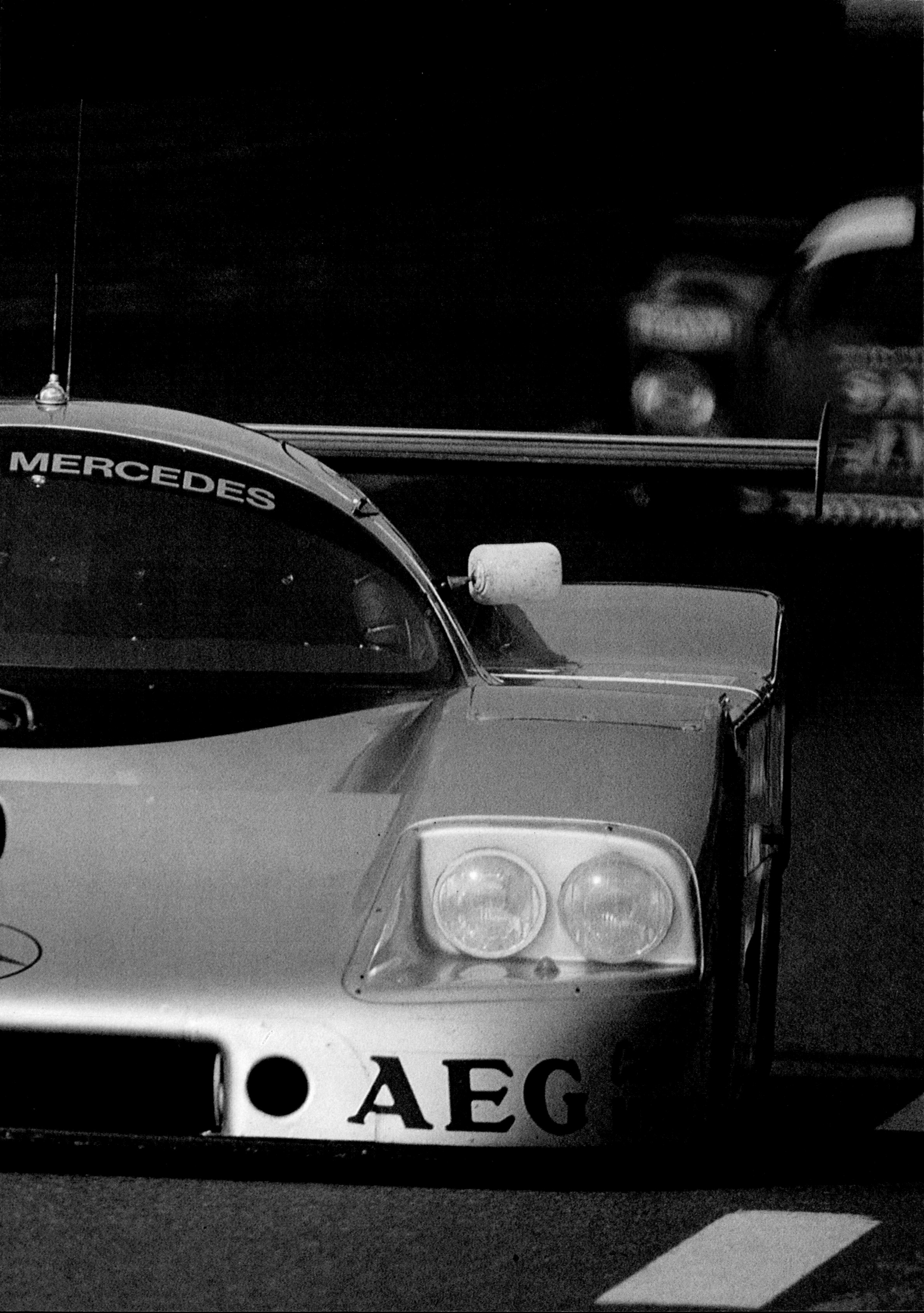
MERCEDES
AEG

*They tell their wives it's only a job. . .*

# STATISTICS

| Position | C1 | C2 | GTP | Drivers | | | Nationality | | | Team | Main Sponsor(s) | No. | Car Type | Engine |
|---|---|---|---|---|---|---|---|---|---|---|---|---|---|---|
| 1 | 1 | | | Stanley Dickens | Jochen Mass | Manuel Reuter | S | D | D | Sauber | Mercedes/AEG | 63 | Sauber C9/88 | 5.0t Mercedes V8 |
| 2 | 2 | | | Kenny Acheson | Mauro Baldi | Gianfranco Brancatelli | GB | I | I | Sauber | Mercedes/AEG | 61 | Sauber C9/88 | 5.0t Mercedes V8 |
| 3 | 3 | | | Hans-Joachim Stuck | Bob Wollek | — | D | F | | Joest | Blaupunkt/Italya | 9 | Porsche 962 | 3.0t Porsche F6 |
| 4 | 4 | | | Jan Lammers | Andrew Gilbert-Scott | Patrick Tambay | NL | GB | F | TWR | Silk Cut/Castrol | 1 | Jaguar XJR9LM | 7.0 Jaguar V12 |
| 5 | 5 | | | Alain Cudini | Jean-Pierre Jabouille | Jean-Louis Schlesser | F | F | F | Sauber | Mercedes/AEG | 62 | Sauber C9/88 | 5.0t Mercedes V8 |
| 6 | 6 | | | Claude Ballot-Lena | Henri Pescarolo | Jean-Louis Ricci | F | F | F | Joest | Blaupunkt/Primagaz | 8 | Porsche 962 | 3.0t Porsche F6 |
| 7 | | | 1 | Pierre Dieudonne | Chris Hodgetts | David Kennedy | B | GB | IRL | Mazda | Finish Line | 201 | Mazda 767B | 1.3r Mazda R4 |
| 8 | 7 | | | Alain Ferte | Michel Ferte | Eliseo Salazar | F | F | RCH | TWR | Silk Cut/Castrol | 4 | Jaguar XJR9LM | 7.0 Jaguar V12 |
| 9 | | | 2 | Herve Regout | Elliott Forbes-Robinson | Takashi Yorino | B | USA | J | Mazda | Charge | 202 | Mazda 767B | 1.3r Mazda R4 |
| 10 | 8 | | | Harald Huysman | Dominique Lacaud | Uwe Schaefer | N | F | D | Brun | Hydro Aluminium | 16 | Porsche 962 | 3.0t Porsche F6 |
| 11 | 9 | | | Costas Los | Brian Redman | Michael Roe | GB | GB | IRL | Aston Martin | Mobil/Proton | 18 | Aston Martin AMR1 | 6.0 Aston Martin V8 |
| 12 | | | 3 | Marc Duez | Yojiro Terada | Volker Weidler | B | J | D | Mazda | Charge | 203 | Mazda 767 | 1.3r Mazda R4 |
| 13 | 10 | 1 | | Gary Brabham | Eje Elgh | Vern Schuppan | AUS | S | AUS | Schuppan | Omron | 55 | Porsche 962 | 3.0t Porsche F6 |
| 14 | | | | Jean-Claude Andruet | Philippe Farjon | Shunji Kasuya | F | F | J | Courage | Laq'alu | 113 | Cougar C20LM | 2.8t Porsche F6 |
| 15 | 11 | 2 | | Tim Lee-Davey | Katsunomi Iketani | Tom Dodd-Noble | GB | J | GB | Davey | Marakatsu | 20 | Porsche 962 | 3.0t Porsche F6 |
| 16 | | 3 | | Ross Hyett | Don Shead | Robbie Stirling | GB | GB | GB | Mako | Curtain Dream | 171 | Spice SE88C | 3.3 Cosworth V8 |
| 17 | | 4 | | Evan Clements | Philippe de Henning | Dudley Wood | GB | F | GB | GPM/RBR | Dianetique | 108 | Spice SE87C | 3.3 Cosworth V8 |
| 18 | | 5 | | Thierry Lecerf | Jean Messaoudi | P-F Rousselot | F | F | F | Prototeam | Speedy | 126 | Argo JM19C | 3.3 Cosworth V8 |
| 19 | | | | J-P Grand | Remy Pouchauvin | Jean-Luc Roy | F | F | F | Graff | Trilles | 104 | Spice SE89C | 3.3 Cosworth V8 |
| R | | | | Derek Bell | Tiff Needell | James Weaver | GB | GB | GB | Lloyd | PCGB/Cabin | 14 | Porsche 962GTi | 3.0t Porsche F6 |
| R | | | | Bruno Giacomelli | Giovanni Lavaggi | Kunimitsu Takahashi | I | I | J | Kremer | Kenwood | 10 | Porsche 962CK6 | 3.0t Porsche F6 |
| R | | | | Geoff Brabham | Arie Luyendyk | Chip Robinson | AUS | NL | USA | Nissan | Nissan | 25 | Nissan R89C | 3.5t Nissan V8 |
| R | | | | Nick Adams | Luigi Taverna | Fermin Velez | GB | I | E | Chamberlain | Repsol/Silk Cut | 101 | Spice SE89C | 3.3 Cosworth V8 |
| R | | | | Walter Brun | Oscar Larrauri | Jesus Pareja | CH | RA | E | Brun | Repsol | 17 | Porsche 962 | 3.0t Porsche F6 |
| R | | | | Ray Bellm | Gordon Spice | Lyn St. James | GB | GB | USA | Spice | Hawaiian Tropic | 21 | Spice SE89C1 | 3.5 Cosworth V8 |
| R | | | | Steven Andskar | Damon Hill | David Hobbs | S | GB | GB | Lloyd | PCGB/Raika | 15 | Porsche 962GTi | 3.0t Porsche F6 |
| R | | | | Akio Morimoto | Anders Olofsson | Takeo Wada | J | S | J | Cougar | Cabin | 32 | March R89V | 3.0t Nissan V8 |
| R | | | | Price Cobb | John Nielsen | Andy Wallace | USA | DK | GB | TWR | Silk Cut/Castrol | 2 | Jaguar XJR9LM | 7.0 Jaguar V12 |
| R | | | | Robin Smith | 'Stingbrace' | Vito Veninata | GB | I | I | Porto Kaleo | Laurent/Perrier | 106 | Tiga GC288 | 3.3 Cosworth V8 |
| R | | | | Jean-Marie Almeras | Jacques Almeras | Alain Ianetta | F | F | I | Almeras | Montpellier | 34 | Porsche 962 | 3.0t Porsche F6 |
| R | | | | Bernard de Dryver | Patrick Gonin | Bernard Santal | B | F | CH | Courage | Simmonds/Faure | 12 | Cougar C22LM | 3.0t Porsche F6 |
| R | | | | Masahiro Hasemi | Kazuyoshi Hoshino | Toshio Suzuki | J | J | J | Nissan | Calsonic | 23 | Nissan R89C | 3.5t Nissan V8 |
| R | | | | David Leslie | Ray Mallock | David Sears | GB | GB | GB | Aston Martin | Mobil/Proton | 19 | Aston Martin AMR1 | 6.0 Aston Martin V8 |
| R | | | | Tim Harvey | Wayne Taylor | Thorkild Thyrring | GB | GB | DK | Spice | FSI/Istel | 22 | Spice SE89C1 | 3.5 Cosworth V8 |
| R | | | | Bernard Thuner | Philippe de Thoisy | Raymond Touroul | CH | F | F | Prototeam | Rexona | 103 | Spice SE88C | 3.3 Cosworth V8 |
| R | | | | Robin Donovan | Max Cohen-Olivar | John Sheldon | GB | MOR | GB | Tiga | JJ/Triples | 107 | Tiga GC289 | 3.3 Cosworth V8 |
| R | | | | Frank Jelinski | P. H. Raphanel | 'John Winter' | D | F | D | Joest | Blaupunkt/Italya | 7 | Porsche 962 | 3.0t Porsche F6 |
| R | | | | Philippe Gaché | Pascal Pessiot | J-D Raulet | F | F | F | WM | Heuliez | 52 | WM P87 | 3.0t Peugeot V6 |
| R | | | | Jean-Louis Bousquet | Pascal Fabre | Jiro Yoneyama | F | F | J | Courage | Simmonds/Leclerc | 13 | Cougar C22LM | 3.0t Porsche F6 |
| R | | | | John Hotchkis Jr. | John Hotchkis Sr. | Richard Jones | USA | USA | GB | Chamberlain | Wynns | 102 | Spice SE86C | 1.8t Hart S4 |
| R | | | | Derek Daly | Davy Jones | Jeff Kline | IRL | USA | USA | TWR | Silk Cut/Castrol | 3 | Jaguar XJR9LM | 7.0 Jaguar V12 |
| R | | | | Franz Konrad | Rudi Seher | Andres Vilarino | A | D | E | Brun | Repsol | 27 | Porsche 962 | 3.0t Porsche F6 |
| R | | | | Harald Grohs | Sarel vd Merwe | Akihiko Nakaya | D | ZA | J | Brun | From-A | 5 | Porsche 962 | 3.0t Porsche F6 |
| R | | | | Louis Descartes | Jacques Heuclin | Alain Serpaggi | F | F | F | Descartes | Liqui Moly | 177 | ALD C289 | 3.3 Cosworth V8 |
| R | | | | Jean Alesi | Dominic Dobson | Will Hoy | F | USA | GB | Schuppan | Takefuji | 33 | Porsche 962 | 3.0t Porsche F6 |
| R | | | | Paul Belmondo | Jurgen Laessig | Pierre Yver | F | D | F | Obermaier | Primagaz | 72 | Porsche 962 | 3.0t Porsche F6 |
| R | | | | Johnny Dumfries | Geoff Lees | John Watson | GB | GB | GB | Toyota | Taka-Q | 37 | Toyota 89CV | 3.2t Toyota V8 |
| R | | | | P-A Lombardi | Fabio Magnini | Bruno Sotty | CH | I | F | Lombardi | GDG | 151 | Spice SE87C | 3.3 Cosworth V8 |
| R | | | | Walter Lechner | R. Ratzenberger | Maurizio Sala | A | A | BR | Brun | Repsol/Alpha | 6 | Porsche 962 | 3.0t Porsche F6 |
| R | | | | Paulo Barilla | Ross Cheever | Hitoshi Ogawa | I | USA | J | Toyota | Minolta | 36 | Toyota 89CV | 3.2t Toyota V8 |
| R | | | | George Fouche | Hideki Okada | Masanori Sekiya | ZA | J | J | Kremer | Leyton House | 11 | Porsche 962CK6 | 3.0t Porsche F6 |
| R | | | | Noel Del Bello | J-C Ferrarin | J-C Justice | CH | F | F | Porto Kaleo | OLIA/Gapstar | 105 | Tiga GC289 | 3.3 Cosworth V8 |
| R | | | | Dider Artzet | Kauro Hoshino | Keiichi Suzuki | F | J | J | Toyota | Nippodenso | 33 | Toyota 88C | 2.1t Toyota S4 |
| R | | | | Laurence Bristow | Ian Harrower | Colin Pool | GB | GB | GB | ADA | CAM/Crawley | 175 | ADA 02 | 3.3 Cosworth V8 |
| R | | | | Julian Bailey | Mark Blundell | Martin Donnelly | GB | GB | GB | Nissan | YHP | 24 | Nissan R89C | 3.5t Nissan V8 |
| R | | | | Roger Dorchy | Philippe Gaché | M Maisonneuve | F | F | F | WM | Heuliez | 51 | WM P88 | 3.0t Peugeot V6 |
| R | | | | Didier Bonnet | Gerard Cuynet | Gerard Tremblay | F | F | F | Bonnet | Le Doubs | 178 | ALD 06 | 3.5 BMW S6 |
| R | | | | Almo Coppelli | Franco Scapini | — | I | I | | Mussato | Frio | 29 | Lancia LC2 | 3.0t Ferrari V8 |
| R | | | | Simon Boulay | Thierry Serfaty | — | F | F | | Descartes | | 176 | ALD 04 | 3.5 BMW S6 |
| R | | | | Francois Cardon | Jean-Luc Colin | — | F | F | | Bonnet | Liqui Moly | 179 | ALD 05 | 3.5 BMW S6 |

| Tyres | Result | Details | Grid Pos | | 1 | 2 | 3 | 4 | 5 | 6 | 7 | 8 | 9 | 10 | 11 | 12 | 13 | 14 | 15 | 16 | 17 | 18 | 19 | 20 | 21 | 22 | 23 | 24 |
|---|---|---|---|---|---|---|---|---|---|---|---|---|---|---|---|---|---|---|---|---|---|---|---|---|---|---|---|---|
| M | 389 laps | 5265.115 kms/219.379 kph | 3-15.04 | 62 | 3 | 3 | 3 | 9 | 9 | 9 | 9 | 9 | 9 | 1 | 1 | 1 | 1 | 1 | 61 | 63 | 63 | 63 | 63 | 63 | 63 | 63 | 63 | 63 |
| M | 384 laps | | 3-15.67 | 61 | 63 | 9 | 9 | 4 | 61 | 7 | 61 | 1 | 1 | 61 | 61 | 61 | 61 | 61 | 63 | 61 | 61 | 61 | 61 | 61 | 61 | 61 | 61 | 61 |
| G | 382 laps | | 3-18.35 | 1 | 9 | 7 | 1 | 7 | 7 | 61 | 1 | 61 | 61 | 63 | 63 | 63 | 63 | 63 | 9 | 9 | 9 | 9 | 9 | 9 | 9 | 9 | 9 | 9 |
| D | 380 laps | | 3-19.48 | 3 | 7 | 1 | 61 | 61 | 23 | 1 | 7 | 23 | 23 | 9 | 2 | 2 | 2 | 9 | 17 | 55 | 55 | 55 | 1 | 62 | 1 | 1 | 1 | 1 |
| M | 378 laps | | 3-19.80 | 9 | 17 | 61 | 7 | 23 | 17 | 4 | 63 | 63 | 2 | 2 | 9 | 4 | 9 | 17 | 55 | 25 | 62 | 1 | 62 | 1 | 62 | 62 | 62 | 62 |
| G | 371 laps | | 3-20.19 | 4 | 62 | 23 | 4 | 1 | 1 | 23 | 23 | 17 | 63 | 23 | 4 | 9 | 17 | 55 | 25 | 62 | 1 | 62 | 55 | 8 | 8 | 8 | 8 | 8 |
| G | 368 laps | 4980.880 kms/207.536 kph | 3-20.26 | 17 | 61 | 62 | 25 | 17 | 4 | 63 | 4 | 2 | 17 | 4 | 17 | 17 | 55 | 25 | 1 | 14 | 14 | 14 | 14 | 14 | 14 | 14 | 201 | 201 |
| D | 368 laps | | 3-20.65 | 2 | 25 | 17 | 17 | 63 | 63 | 17 | 17 | 4 | 4 | 17 | 25 | 25 | 25 | 14 | 62 | 1 | 8 | 8 | 8 | 201 | 201 | 201 | 4 | 4 |
| G | 365 laps | | 3-21.51 | 5 | 1 | 4 | 23 | 25 | 2 | 2 | 2 | 25 | 15 | 15 | 55 | 55 | 14 | 15 | 14 | 8 | 201 | 201 | 201 | 202 | 202 | 202 | 202 | 202 |
| Y | 351 laps | | 3-22.70 | 11 | 23 | 25 | 6 | 8 | 55 | 55 | 25 | 7 | 8 | 25 | 14 | 14 | 15 | 2 | 8 | 201 | 202 | 202 | 202 | 10 | 4 | 4 | 16 | 16 |
| G | 340 laps | | 3-22.86 | 63 | 33 | 33 | 63 | 2 | 15 | 15 | 15 | 8 | 25 | 14 | 15 | 15 | 8 | 62 | 15 | 202 | 10 | 10 | 10 | 4 | 16 | 16 | 203 | 18 |
| G | 339 laps | | 3-24.09 | 24 | 37 | 8 | 8 | 15 | 202 | 25 | 8 | 15 | 202 | 55 | 8 | 8 | 62 | 8 | 201 | 17 | 4 | 4 | 4 | 55 | 55 | 55 | 18 | 203 |
| G | 321 laps | | 3-24.77 | 7 | 8 | 14 | 55 | 202 | 8 | 8 | 202 | 202 | 55 | 202 | 202 | 62 | 201 | 202 | 202 | 10 | 16 | 16 | 16 | 16 | 18 | 203 | 55 | 55 |
| G | 312 laps | 4222.920 kms/175.955 kph | 3-24.92 | 10 | 4 | 6 | 10 | 25 | 201 | 201 | 13 | 14 | 14 | 8 | 62 | 201 | 202 | 201 | 10 | 4 | 101 | 18 | 18 | 18 | 203 | 18 | 113 | 113 |
| D | 308 laps | | 3-25.38 | 25 | 6 | 5 | 15 | 62 | 25 | 202 | 14 | 201 | 201 | 201 | 23 | 202 | 4 | 10 | 203 | 16 | 17 | 203 | 203 | 203 | 113 | 113 | 171 | 20 |
| G | 307 laps | | 3-25.45 | 202 | 202 | 202 | 14 | 201 | 13 | 13 | 201 | 55 | 62 | 62 | 201 | 10 | 10 | 4 | 16 | 203 | 18 | 101 | 113 | 113 | 171 | 171 | 20 | 171 |
| G | 303 laps | | 3-25.60 | 37 | 5 | 2 | 13 | 13 | 14 | 14 | 55 | 34 | 12 | 10 | 10 | 21 | 101 | 16 | 4 | 101 | 203 | 17 | 101 | 171 | 20 | 20 | 108 | 108 |
| G | 297 laps | | 3-26.89 | 55 | 14 | 37 | 202 | 14 | 12 | 12 | 34 | 62 | 34 | 34 | 34 | 34 | 203 | 203 | 101 | 21 | 126 | 126 | 17 | 20 | 126 | 126 | 126 | 126 |
| G | 291 laps | | 3-26.95 | 23 | 10 | 13 | 2 | 12 | 34 | 19 | 19 | 10 | 10 | 21 | 21 | 101 | 16 | 101 | 32 | 15 | 113 | 113 | 126 | 108 | 108 | 104 | 104 | |
| G | 339 laps | Fire | 3-27.07 | 6 | 6 | 63 | 37 | 21 | 19 | 34 | 62 | 19 | 19 | 19 | 12 | 203 | 34 | 21 | 2 | 18 | 2 | 171 | 171 | 108 | 104 | 104 | | |
| Y | 303 laps | Fire | 3-27.75 | 14 | 27 | 10 | 201 | 203 | 21 | 62 | 203 | 12 | 21 | 101 | 203 | 16 | 21 | 32 | 21 | 32 | 20 | 20 | 20 | 101 | | | | |
| D | 250 laps | Engine | 3-27.79 | 33 | 101 | 55 | 12 | 76 | 203 | 101 | 101 | 101 | 101 | 12 | 101 | 32 | 32 | 18 | 18 | 126 | 171 | 108 | 108 | 104 | | | | |
| G | 244 laps | Engine | 3-27.97 | 15 | 13 | 15 | 21 | 34 | 101 | 203 | 10 | 203 | 203 | 203 | 16 | 18 | 18 | 126 | 126 | 2 | 108 | 104 | 104 | 52 | | | | |
| Y | 242 laps | Engine | 3-28.32 | 36 | 15 | 201 | 62 | 10 | 18 | 21 | 21 | 21 | 32 | 32 | 32 | 12 | 126 | 113 | 113 | 113 | 106 | 106 | 106 | | | | | |
| G | 229 laps | Engine | 3-28.64 | 38 | 12 | 12 | 27 | 101 | 62 | 16 | 32 | 18 | 16 | 16 | 18 | 126 | 104 | 106 | 106 | 106 | 106 | 104 | 52 | 52 | | | | |
| G | 228 laps | Engine | 3-29.41 | 27 | 36 | 36 | 101 | 19 | 16 | 18 | 12 | 32 | 126 | 18 | 19 | 104 | 12 | 104 | 20 | 171 | 52 | | | | | | | |
| Y | 221 laps | Engine | 3-29.90 | 16 | 72 | 22 | 203 | 18 | 10 | 32 | 18 | 16 | 18 | 126 | 126 | 113 | 113 | 20 | 171 | 20 | | | | | | | | |
| D | 215 laps | Engine | 3-31.38 | 201 | 201 | 72 | 72 | 16 | 32 | 10 | 104 | 13 | 113 | 113 | 104 | 106 | 106 | 171 | 108 | 108 | | | | | | | | |
| G | 194 laps | Electrics | 3-31.49 | 13 | 22 | 27 | 34 | 32 | 104 | 104 | 16 | 126 | 104 | 104 | 113 | 20 | 20 | 108 | 104 | 104 | | | | | | | | |
| G | 188 laps | Accident | 3-32.00 | 72 | 21 | 21 | 36 | 37 | 5 | 3 | 126 | 113 | 106 | 106 | 106 | 171 | 171 | 22 | 22 | 22 | | | | | | | | |
| G | 168 laps | Electrics | 3-32.54 | 21 | 151 | 101 | 19 | 104 | 27 | 126 | 103 | 104 | 13 | 20 | 20 | 108 | 108 | 52 | 52 | 52 | | | | | | | | |
| D | 167 laps | Engine | 3-34.08 | 18 | 104 | 203 | 18 | 33 | 126 | 106 | 113 | 103 | 103 | 107 | 107 | 103 | 103 | | | | | | | | | | | |
| G | 153 laps | Engine | 3-35.42 | 8 | 55 | 34 | 32 | 106 | 106 | 27 | 106 | 106 | 107 | 103 | 103 | 107 | 107 | | | | | | | | | | | |
| G | 150 laps | Engine | 3-36.69 | 203 | 20 | 18 | 104 | 27 | 33 | 113 | 171 | 171 | 171 | 108 | 108 | 22 | 22 | | | | | | | | | | | |
| G | 133 laps | Transmission | 3-36.91 | 34 | 38 | 104 | 16 | 126 | 3 | 103 | 107 | 20 | 20 | 171 | 171 | 177 | 52 | | | | | | | | | | | |
| G | 126 laps | Transmission | 3-38.47 | 22 | 34 | 20 | 113 | 151 | 113 | 5 | 20 | 107 | 108 | 22 | 22 | 52 | | | | | | | | | | | | |
| G | 124 laps | Engine | 3-38.70 | 104 | 203 | 19 | 106 | 5 | 103 | 171 | 102 | 102 | 102 | 177 | 177 | | | | | | | | | | | | | |
| M | 110 laps | Fire | 3-38.74 | 12 | 103 | 32 | 126 | 113 | 171 | 107 | 108 | 108 | 22 | 52 | 52 | | | | | | | | | | | | | |
| G | 110 laps | Engine | 3-39.91 | 32 | 18 | 171 | 33 | 3 | 107 | 33 | 151 | 22 | 177 | | | | | | | | | | | | | | | |
| G | 86 laps | Engine | 3-40.11 | 19 | 177 | 126 | 103 | 103 | 37 | 102 | 137 | 177 | 52 | | | | | | | | | | | | | | | |
| D | 85 laps | Engine | 3-41.04 | 101 | 113 | 113 | 151 | 107 | 151 | 20 | 22 | 151 | | | | | | | | | | | | | | | | |
| Y | 81 laps | Engine | 3-41.94 | 151 | 32 | 106 | 5 | 171 | 102 | 37 | 52 | 52 | | | | | | | | | | | | | | | | |
| Y | 78 laps | Electrics | 3-42.31 | 20 | 126 | 16 | 22 | 6 | 20 | 151 | 175 | 175 | | | | | | | | | | | | | | | | |
| G | 75 laps | Electrics | 3-44.00 | 52 | 106 | 151 | 11 | 102 | 108 | 108 | | | | | | | | | | | | | | | | | | |
| G | 69 laps | Fire | 3-44.44 | 103 | 171 | 103 | 107 | 36 | 22 | 177 | | | | | | | | | | | | | | | | | | |
| G | 61 laps | Accident | 3-44.99 | 102 | 52 | 108 | 171 | 11 | 105 | 22 | | | | | | | | | | | | | | | | | | |
| B | 58 laps | Accident | 3-45.45 | 171 | 19 | 107 | 102 | 22 | 177 | 105 | | | | | | | | | | | | | | | | | | |
| G | 58 laps | Accident | 3-45.86 | 113 | 16 | 105 | 177 | 20 | 52 | 52 | | | | | | | | | | | | | | | | | | |
| Y | 50 laps | Accident | 3-46.23 | 108 | 107 | 102 | 20 | 108 | 175 | 175 | | | | | | | | | | | | | | | | | | |
| B | 45 laps | Engine | 3-47.03 | 107 | 105 | 11 | 108 | 177 | | | | | | | | | | | | | | | | | | | | |
| Y | 42 laps | Accident | 3-48.27 | 106 | 102 | 177 | 105 | 105 | | | | | | | | | | | | | | | | | | | | |
| G | 36 laps | Engine | 3-48.80 | 175 | 108 | 52 | 52 | 52 | | | | | | | | | | | | | | | | | | | | |
| B | 20 laps | Accident | 3-50.37 | 126 | 175 | 38 | 38 | 38 | | | | | | | | | | | | | | | | | | | | |
| G | 14 laps | Electrics | 3-50.82 | 105 | 11 | 175 | 175 | 175 | | | | | | | | | | | | | | | | | | | | |
| D | 5 laps | Accident | 3-55.36 | 177 | 24 | 24 | | | | | | | | | | | | | | | | | | | | | | |
| M | DNS | Fire | | | | | | | | | | | | | | | | | | | | | | | | | | |
| A | DNS | DNQ | | | | | | | | | | | | | | | | | | | | | | | | | | |
| D | DNS | DNQ | | | | | | | | | | | | | | | | | | | | | | | | | | |
| G | DNS | DNQ | | | | | | | | | | | | | | | | | | | | | | | | | | |
| A | DNS | DNQ | | | | | | | | | | | | | | | | | | | | | | | | | | |

Length of circuit: = 13.535km/8.412 miles
(unaltered from last year)

Fastest laps:
Alain Ferte 3m21.27s/242.093kph/150.429 mph/Record

Tyres: A = Avon
B = Bridgestone
D = Dunlop
G = Goodyear
M = Michelin
Y = Yokohama

Acknowledgements:

**MERCEDES MAGIC –**
The Story Of The 1989 Le Mans Race.

**WRITTEN** by Ken Wells

**ADDITIONAL FEATURES** by
John Allen
Mike Cotton

**AIRBRUSH ILLUSTRATIONS** by
Rosemary Hutchings

**CHIEF PHOTOGRAPHERS:**
John Allen
Jeff Bloxham
Malcolm Bryan
Stephen Payne
Ken Wells

**ADDITIONAL MATERIAL** by
Lyn Chalk
David Connell
Gordon Dawkins
Geoff Knight
Lesley Knight
Alan Stacey
Peter Woods
Nissan Proteus/CTP

**PLEASE NOTE** that most of the photographers have given
their services free of charge, their fees being donated to the
Foundation for the Study of Infant Death.

**SPECIAL THANKS** to
All staff and officials of
Daytona International Speedway
The ACO, Le Mans
Silverstone/Brands Hatch/Donington
also
Barry and Lindsey Bass
Mark Bridges
Bob Cowper
Alan and 'Roni' Collins
Wyn Edwards
Bob Elson
Paul and Janice Minton
Jim and Jeanne Stanton
My Mum!

**PUBLISHED** by
Prancing Tortoise Publications
4, Highfield Rise,
Althorne, Chelmsford,
Essex, CM3 6DN.

(Telephone 0621 741153)

in consultation with
First Avenue Publishing Limited.

**EDITOR/CONSULTANT:** Lee Thomas (FAP)

**DESIGN:** Rosemary Hutchings/Ken Wells

**TYPESETTING:** Fleetlines Limited, Southend-on-Sea

**ARTWORK/REPRO:** Hilo Offset Limited, Colchester

**PRINTED** in Portsmouth by MacLehose & Partners Limited

**FIRST PUBLISHED:** November 1989

ISBN: 0 9515382 0 9

Illustrations

Sauber Mercedes C9 – prints now available

## rd illustrations

Airbrush illustrations

Decal design

Logos

Promotional visuals

`The Croft´
32 Oaklands Close
West Kingsdown
Kent TN15 6EA
England

West Kingsdown·3793

Design & Illustration

Photography

Line drawing

Camera ready artwork

For free quotations and information on prints
please contact –
**Rosemary or Alan on 047485 3793**

Illustrations

**Proprietors : Rosemary Hutchings - Alan Stacey**

127